# A LITTLE BOOK OF ETERNAL WISDOM

HENRY SUSO

SSEL

# CONTENTS

*A FOREWORD* vii
*THE PARABLE OF THE PILGRIM* xi
*TRANSLATOR'S NOTE* xxi
*BLESSED HENRY SUSO'S PREFACE TO HIS BOOK* xxiii

## PART THE FIRST

1. How Some Persons Are Unconsciously Attracted By God — 3
2. What Happened Before The Crucifixion — 8
3. How It Was With Him On The Cross According To The Exterior Man — 14
4. How Very Faithful His Passion Was — 17
5. How The Soul Attains Hearty Repentance and Gentle Pardon Under the Cross — 20
6. How Deceitful The Love Of This World Is, And How Amiable God Is — 28
7. How Lovely God Is — 38
8. An Explanation — 47
9. The Second Thing. — 50
10. The Third Thing. — 58
11. On The Everlasting Pains of Hell — 61
12. On The Immeasurable Joys of Heaven — 66

13. On The Immeasurable Dignity of Temporal Suffering — 76
14. On The Unspeakable Advantages to Be Derived From Meditating on The Divine Passion — 85
15. From The Fond Caresses — 92
16. On The Worthy Praise of The Pure Queen of Heaven — 98
17. On The Unutterable Heart-Rending Grief of The Pure Queen of Heaven — 106
18. How It Was With Him At That Hour in Regard of His Interior Man — 113
19. On The Taking Down From the Cross — 118
20. On The Lamentable Separation of the Grave — 123

## THE SECOND PART

1. How We Should Learn to Die, And of The Nature of An Unprovided Death — 127
2. How One Should Live An Interior and Godly Life — 141
3. How We Ought Lovingly To Receive God — 144
4. A Prayer To Be Said When Thou Goest To Receive Our Lord's Holy Body — 162
5. How We Should At All Times Praise God — 164

# THE THIRD PART
## ONE HUNDRED MEDITATIONS AND PRAYERS, COMPRISED IN FEW WORDS.

| | |
|---|---|
| On Sunday, Or At Matins | 183 |
| On Monday, Or At Prime | 186 |
| On Tuesday, Or At Tierce | 188 |
| On Wednesday, Or At Sext | 190 |
| On Thursday, Or At None | 193 |
| On Friday, Or At Vespers | 195 |
| On Saturday, Or At Compline | 197 |

# A FOREWORD

Jesus and Mary! Sacred names, always united in the mind and heart of every true Christian. Jesus, model of true manhood; Mary, model of true womanhood. Jesus, begotten of the Father before all ages, the figure of His substance, by whom were made all things that were made. Mary, first woman in the mind of the Creator; original type, remaining unfallen when every copy fell! Woman, destined from eternity to crush the head of the unclean demon. Jesus and Mary! Models of the interior life, to you is dedicated this new edition of a work of one of your devoted servants, which is well calculated to lead many souls up the path of perfection till they reign with you in the Kingdom of Heaven.

The LITTLE BOOK OF ETERNAL

WISDOM is among the best of the writings of Blessed Henry Suso, a priest of the Order of St. Dominic, who lived a life of wonderful labours and sufferings, and died in the Fourteenth century with a reputation for sanctity which the Church has solemnly confirmed. Gregory XVI granted to the whole Order of St. Dominic the privilege of celebrating his office, and of offering the Mass yearly in his honour, appointing the Second of March for his festival.

The Order of St. Dominic, known in the Church both as the Order of Truth and the Order of Preachers, so rich in pontiffs, martyrs, and confessors, is also illustrious for its theologians, its ascetic writers, its great masters of the spiritual life. Its mystic theologians stand in the first rank of those who have scaled the wondrous heights of sublime perfection. Not only have they stood on the mountain tops of the spiritual life, but they have pointed out, with a clearness surpassed by no other writers, the path of ascent, marking for the unwary its every danger. The wiles of the enemy are exposed; where, when, and how he seeks to accomplish our ruin. Our defence is first outlined, and then given in detail. The source of strength is pointed out, and thus the perilous journey may safely be made.

Among the ascetic writers of the Order, mention may be made of St. Thomas Aquinas, Blessed

Albert the Great, Master Humbert, St. Antoninus, Dom Bartholomew of the Martyrs, Ven. Louis of Granada, St. Vincent Ferrer, St. Catherine of Sienna, and St. Catherine of Ricci, whilst the Illuminated Doctor John Tauler and Blessed Henry Suso are among the first of the great mystic theologians of the Church.

THE LITTLE BOOK OF ETERNAL WISDOM was translated and published for the Catholics of England years ago, but has long been out of print. It would be difficult to speak too highly of this little book or of its author. In soundness of teaching, sublimity of thought, clearness of expression, and beauty of illustration, we do not know of a spiritual writer that surpasses Henry Suso. He clothes virtue in such lovely garments, the path to the sublime heights of perfection is so clearly marked out, that the willing soul is allured onward and assisted upward, till she stands with her blessed guide in the full light of the Eternal Wisdom.

To this preface it was deemed advisable to add the celebrated "Parable of the Pilgrim," taken from the writings of Walter Hilton, a Carthusian monk, and afterwards abridged by the venerable contemplative Father Baker, of the Order of St. Benedict.

The devout reader is earnestly requested to read this parable again and again before commencing the study of Suso's golden book of Eternal Wisdom. This parable outlines the whole plan of the spiritual life, it conveys most useful instructions for those who seriously aim at perfection, which Hilton designates as the Vision of Peace given to the Soul in Jerusalem. This parable will be understood and appreciated by those only who are hungering after Justice. They should read it frequently, and fervently pray for grace to become true pilgrims and pursue the path here clearly marked out, that so they may arrive at the glorious end.

C. H. McKenna, O.P.

# THE PARABLE OF THE PILGRIM

A certain man had a great desire to go to Jerusalem. Not knowing the right way, he inquired of one he hoped could direct him, and asked by what path he could reach there in safety. The other said, "The journey there is long and full of difficulties. There are several roads that appear and promise to lead there, but their dangers are too great. However, I know one way which, if you will faithfully follow according to the marks and directions that I shall give you, will certainly lead you there. I cannot, however, promise you security from many frights, beatings, and other ill-usages and temptations of all kinds, yet if you only have courage and patience enough to suffer them without quarrelling, or resisting, or troubling yourself about them, but pass on quietly, having this only in your mind, and sometimes on you tongue, 'I have naught, I am naught, I desire naught but to be in Jerusalem,' my life for yours, in due time you will get there in safety."

The pilgrim, full of joy at the news said, "If only I arrive at length in safety at the place I desire so much, I care not what miseries I suffer on the way; therefore, only let me know the course I am to take, and, God willing, I shall not fail carefully to observe all your directions."—"Since you have so good a will," said the guide, "though I myself was never so happy as to be in Jerusalem, yet be assured that if you follow the instructions I shall give, you will arrive safe at the end of your journey."

The advice is briefly this: Before taking the first step on the highway that leads there you must be firmly grounded in the truths of the Catholic faith. Moreover, whatever sins you find sullying your conscience you must cleanse by hearty penance and absolution according to the laws of the Church. Having done so begin your journey in God's name; but be sure to have with you two necessary instruments, Humility and Charity. These are contained in the words above mentioned, which must always be present to your mind, "I am naught, I have naught, I desire only one thing and that is our Lord Jesus, and to be with Him at peace in Jerusalem." The meaning and power of these words you must have continually, at least in your thoughts either expressly or virtually. Humility says, "I am nothing, I have nothing." Charity says, "I desire nothing but Jesus." You must never lose these two companions, neither will they consent to be separated from each other, for they agree lovingly together, and the deeper you establish yourself in humility the higher you will advance in charity, for the more you see and feel yourself to be nothing the more ardently you will see and love Jesus, that by Him who is All you may become something.

This humility is to be exercised not so much in considering your own vileness and sinfulness, though in the beginning this consideration is good and beneficial, but rather in a quiet consideration of the infinite being and goodness of Jesus. You are to behold Him either through grace in sensible devotional knowledge of Him, or, at least, in a full and firm faith in Him. And such a contemplation of the infinite sanctity and goodness of Jesus will operate in your mind a much more pure, spiritual, solid and perfect humility, than the reflecting on your own nothingness, which produces a humility much more gross, boisterous and imperfect. In this mirror of sanctity you will behold yourself to be not only the most wretched, filthy creature in the world, but also, in the very substance of your soul, setting aside the foulness of sin, to be a mere nothing; for really, in comparison with Jesus who is All, you are nothing. And until you have and feel that you have the love of Jesus, although you think you have done ever so many good deeds, spiritually and worldly, you have nothing, for nothing but the love of Jesus will abide in and fill your soul. Therefore cast aside and forget all other things in order that you may have that which is the best of all. If you do this you will become a true pilgrim, who leaves behind him house, wife, children, friends, and goods, and denies himself all things in order that he may go on his journey lightly and without hindrance.

If your desire for Jesus still continues and grows stronger, so that you go on your way courageously, they will then tell you that you may become ill, and perhaps with such a disease as will bring frightful dreads into your mind; or perhaps you will become very poor and you will find no charitable person to help you. Do not heed what they say, but if you should happen to fall into sickness or poverty, still have faith in Jesus, and say, "I am naught, I have naught, I care for naught in this world, and I desire naught but the love of Jesus, that I may see Him at peace in Jerusalem."

If it should ever happen that through some of these temptations and your own weakness, you waver and perhaps fall into sin, and thus lose the way for a time, return as soon as possible to the right path by using such remedies as the Church ordains. Do not think of your past sins, for that will harm you and favour your enemies; but make haste to go on your way as if nothing happened. Think only of Jesus, and of your desire to gain His love, and nothing will harm you.

Finally, when your enemies see that you are so determined that neither sickness, fancies, poverty, life, death, nor sins discourage you, but that you will continue to seek the love of Jesus and nothing else, by continuing your prayer and other spiritual works, they will grow enraged and will not spare you the most cruel abuse. They will make their most dangerous assault by bringing before you all your good deeds and virtues, showing that all men praise, love, and honour you for your sanctity. This they will do to make you vain and proud. But if you offer your life to Jesus you will consider all this flattery and falsehood as deadly poison to your soul, and will cast it from you.

In order to shun such temptations renounce all vain thoughts and think of Jesus only, resolving to know and love Him. After you have accustomed yourself to think of Him alone, any thoughts not relating to Him will be unwelcome and painful to you.

If there is any work you are obliged to do for yourself or neighbour fail not to do it as soon and as well as you can, lest by delay it may distract your thoughts from Jesus. If it is unnecessary work do not think about it, but dismiss it from your thoughts saying, "I am naught, I can do naught, I have naught, and I desire naught but Jesus and His love."

It will be necessary for you, as for all other pilgrims, to take, on the way, sleep and refreshments and sometimes innocent recreation; but if you use discretion in these things, although they seem to delay you, they will give you strength and courage to continue on your journey.

To conclude, remember that your principal aim, and indeed only business, is to give your thoughts to the desire of Jesus, and to strengthen this desire by daily prayer and other spiritual works. And whatever you find suitable to increase that desire, be it praying or reading, speaking or being silent, working or resting, make use of it as long as your soul finds delight in it, and as long as it increases the desire of having and enjoying nothing but the love of Jesus and the blessed sight of Jesus in true peace in Jerusalem. Be assured that this good desire, thus cherished and continually increased, will bring you safely to the end of your pilgrimage.

Observing these instructions, you are in the

right path to Jerusalem. To proceed on this journey, it is necessary to do, inwardly and outwardly, such works as are suitable to your condition, and such as will help to increase in you the gracious desire that you have to love Jesus only. No matter what your works are, whether thinking, reading, preaching, labouring, etc., if you find that they draw your mind from worldly vanity and strengthen your heart and will more to the love of Jesus, it is good and profitable for you to pursue them. But if through custom, you find such works in time lose their power and virtue to increase this love, cast them aside and try some other works which you think will gain for you more grace and sanctity; for, although the inclination and desire of your heart for Jesus should never change, nevertheless the spiritual works you practice, such as prayer, reading, etc., in order to feed and strengthen this desire, may well be changed, according as you feel your spiritual welfare will be benefited by this change. Therefore, lest you hinder the freedom of your heart to love Jesus, do not think that because you have accustomed yourself to a certain form of devotion, that you cannot change it for a better.

Before you have journeyed far, you must expect enemies of all kinds, who will surround you and busily endeavour to hinder you from going forward. Indeed, if they can by any means, they will, either by persuasions, flatteries, or violence, force you to return to your former habits of sinfulness. For there is nothing annoys them so much as to see a resolute desire to love Jesus and to labour to find him. Consequently, they will conspire to drive out of your heart that good desire and love in which all virtues are comprised. The first enemies that will assault you will be the desires of the flesh, and vain fears of your corrupt heart. Joined with these will be unclean spirits, which, with sights and temptations, will seek to entice you to them, and draw you from Jesus. But do not believe anything they say, but betake yourself to your old and only secure remedy, answering—"I am naught, I have naught, and I desire naught but only the love of Jesus."

If they endeavour to put dreads and doubts into your mind, and try to make you believe you have not done necessary penance to atone for your sins, do not believe them. Neither believe them if they say you have not sufficiently confessed your sins, and that you should return home to do penance better, before you have the boldness to go to Jesus. You are sufficiently acquitted of your sins, and there is no need at all that you should delay in order to ransack your conscience, for this will now but harm you, and either put you entirely out of your way, or at least unprofitably delay your toil.

If they tell you that you are not worthy to have the love of Jesus, or to see Jesus, and that on that account you ought not to be so presumptuous as to desire and seek it, do not believe them, but go on, saying, "It is not because I am worthy, but because I am unworthy, that I desire to have the love of Jesus; for, once having that, I should become worthy. Therefore, I will never cease desiring it until I have obtained it. I was created for this love alone, and so, say and do what you will, I will desire it continually, and never cease to pray for it, and thus endeavour to obtain it."

If you meet with any who seem to be your friends, and who in kindness would hinder your progress by entertaining you and seeking to draw you to sensual mirth by vain discourses and carnal pleasures, whereby you will be in danger of forgetting your pilgrimage, turn a deaf ear to them, answer them not; think only of this, that you would fain be at Jerusalem. If they offer you gifts and attractions, heed them not, but think ever of Jerusalem.

If men despise you, lay false charges against you, defraud and rob you, or even beat and use you cruelly, for your life take no notice of them, but meekly content yourself with the injury received, and proceed as if nothing had happened to hinder you. This punishment, or even more, is as nothing if you can only arrive at Jerusalem, where you shall be recompensed for all you have endured.

If your enemies see that you grow courageous, and that you will neither be seduced by flatteries nor disheartened by the pains and trials of your journey, but rather are contented with them, they will then be afraid of you. Notwithstanding all this, they will still pursue you on your way and seek every advantage against you, now and then endeavouring, either by flatteries or alarms, to stop and drive you back. Fear them not, but continue on your way thinking of nothing but Jerusalem and Jesus, whom you will find there.

Walter Hilton,<br>Canon of Thurgarton

# TRANSLATOR'S NOTE

This edition of Blessed Henry Suso's Little Book of Eternal Wisdom is translated from the classical German text of Cardinal Melchior Diepenbrock, Prince-Bishop of Breslau.

That it is a very imperfect reproduction of the incomparable original, I am fully aware, but there are authors whose beauties of idiom are such as to be untranslatable, and Suso is one of them.

It is superfluous to enlarge here on the intrinsic merits of Blessed Henry Suso's work. For over five hundred years it has enjoyed undiminished popularity, as at once a religious and literary masterpiece. Such a work speaks too eloquently for itself; it is its own best praise, its own best commentary.

# BLESSED HENRY SUSO'S PREFACE TO HIS BOOK

A preacher once stood, after matins, before a crucifix, and complained from his heart to God that he could not meditate properly on His torments and passion, and that this was very bitter for him, inasmuch as, up to that hour, he had in consequence suffered so much. And, as he thus stood with his complaint, his interior senses were rapt to an unusual exaltation, in which he was very speedily and clearly enlightened as follows: Thou shalt make a hundred *venias*,\* and each *venia* with a special meditation of My passion, and each meditation with a request. And every one of My sufferings shall be spiritually im-

---

\* A form of prostration, "at full length on the right side," practiced by the Dominicans.

pressed on thee, to suffer the same again through Me as far as thou art able.

And as he thus stood in the light, and would needs count the *venias,* he only found ninety, upon which he spoke to God thus: Sweet Lord, Thou didst speak of a hundred *venias,* and I find only ninety. Then he was reminded of ten others which he had already made in the Chapter House, before solemnizing, according to his custom, the devout meditation of the miserable leading forth of Christ to death, and coming before that very crucifix; and so he found that the hundred meditations had entirely included from beginning to end His bitter Passion and death. And when he began to exercise himself in this matter, as he had been directed, his former dryness was changed into an interior sweetness.

Now it was his request that if, perchance, any one else had the same imperfection, and felt the same dryness and bitterness in meditating on Christ's Passion in which all sanctification lies, he too might be assisted, and might exercise himself therein, and not desist until he had attained salvation. And, therefore, he wrote his mediations down, and wrote them in German, because he had so received them from God. Accordingly, he gained many a bright inspiration of divine truth, whereof these meditations were a cause, and between him and the Eternal Wisdom there sprang up a tender intercourse, and this took place not by a bodily intercourse nor by figurative answers; it took place solely by meditation in the light of Holy Writ whose answers can deceive in nothing; so that the answers are taken either from the mouth of the Eternal Wisdom who uttered them herself in the Gospel, or else from the highest doctors, and they comprise either the same words or the same sense, or else such truths as are agreeable to Holy Writ, out of whose mouth the Eternal Wisdom spoke. Nor did the visions which hereafter follow take place in a bodily way; they are but an interpreted similitude.

The answer touching our Blessed Lady's complaint he has given in the sense of St. Bernard's words; and the reason why he propounds his doctrine by question and answer is that it may prove the more attractive; that it may not seem as though he were the person to whom the doctrine belonged, or who had spoken it as coming from himself. His object is to give a general doctrine, in which he and all persons may find every one what is suitable for himself. He takes upon himself, as a teacher ought to do, the person of all mankind: now he speaks in the person of a sinner; now under the image of a love-sick soul; then, as the matter suggests, in the likeness of a servant with whom the Eternal Wisdom discourses. Moreover, everything is expounded with reference to our interior; much is given here as doctrine that a zealous man should choose out for himself as devout prayer. The thoughts which stand here are simple, the words simpler still, for they proceed from a simple soul and are meant for simple men who have still their imperfections to cast aside.

It happened that, as the same brother had begun to write on the three matters, namely, the Passion, and the rest of it all, and had come to that part on repentance: *Now then, cheer up thou soul of mine! etc.*, he had reclined himself one forenoon on his chair, and that in a bright sleep he saw clearly, in a vision, how two culpable persons sat before him, and how he chastised them very severely for sitting there so idly, and performing nothing. Then was it given him to understand that he should thread a needle, which was put into his hand. Now the thread was threefold; and two parts were very fine, but the other part was a little coarser, and when he would needs twist the three together he could not well do it. Then he saw close to him on his right hand our Lord, standing the same as when He was unbound from the pillar, and He stood before him with a look so kind and fatherly that he thought it was indeed his father. Now he perceived that His body had quite a natural colour; it was not very white, but of the colour of wheat, that is, white and red well mixed together (and this is the most natural colour of all), and he perceived that His whole body was covered with wounds, and that they were quite fresh and bloody, that some were round, some angular, some very long, just as the whips had torn Him; and as He thus stood sweetly before him, and kindly looked at him, the preacher raised his hands and rubbed them to and fro on His bloody wounds, and then took the three parts of the thread and twisted them easily together. Then was given to him a power, and he understood that he was to complete his task, and that God with His rose-coloured garment (which is wrought so delightfully out of His wounds) would clothe all those in eternal beauty who should occupy their time and leisure with it here below.

One thing, however, a man should know, that there is as great a difference between hearing himself the sweet accords of a harp and hearing another speak of them, as there is between the words received in pure grace and that flow out of a living heart, through a living mouth, and those same words when they come to be set down on dead parchment, especially in the German tongue; for then are they chilled, and they wither like plucked roses: for the sprightliness of their delivery, which, more than anything, moves the heart of man, is then extinguished, and in the dryness of dry hearts are they received. Never was there a string how sweet soever, but it became dumb when stretched on a dry log. A joyless heart can as little understand a joyful tongue as a German can an Englishman! Therefore let every fervent soul hasten after the first out-pourings of this sweet doctrine, so that she may learn to contemplate them in their origin, where they were in all their loveliness and ravishing beauty; even there are the in-pourings of the present grace, to the quickening of hearts that are dead! And he who thus looks at this book will hardly have read it through before his heart will needs be deeply moved either to fervent love, or to new light, or to a yearning towards God, and abhorrence of sin, or else to some spiritual request, wherein the soul will presently be renewed in grace.

*Here ends the Preface, and follows*

# PART THE FIRST

# 1
# HOW SOME PERSONS ARE UNCONSCIOUSLY ATTRACTED BY GOD

*Her have I loved, and have sought her out from my youth, and have desired to take her for my spouse, and I became a lover of her beauty.* These words stand written in the Book of Wisdom\* and are spoken by the beautiful and all-loving Wisdom.

*A Servant* was filled with disgust and dejection of heart on his first setting forth on the uneven ways. Then did the Eternal Wisdom meet him in a spiritual and ineffable form, and lead him through bitter and sweet until she brought him to the right path of divine truth. And after well reflecting on his wonderful progress, he thus spoke to God: Sweet and tender Lord! from the days of

---
\* viii.2

my childhood my mind has sought for something with burning thirst, but what it is I have not as yet fully understood. Lord, I have pursued it ardently many a year, but I never could grasp it, for I know not what it is, and yet it is something that attracts my heart and soul, without which I never can attain true rest. Lord, I sought it in the first days of my childhood, as I saw done around me, in creatures, but the more I sought it in them the less I found it, and the nearer I approached them the further I receded from it, for every image that presented itself to my sight, before I wholly tried it, or gave myself up quietly to it, warned me away thus: "I am not what thou seekest!" And this repulsion I have experienced more and more in all things. Lord, now my heart rages after it, for my heart would so gladly possess it. Alas! I have so constantly had to experience what it is not! But what it is, Lord, I am not as yet clear. Tell me, beloved Lord, what it is indeed, and what is its nature, that so secretly agitates me.

*Answer of Eternal Wisdom.*—Dost thou not know it? And yet it has lovingly embraced thee, has often stopped thee in the way, until it has at length won thee for itself alone.

*The Servant.*—Lord, I never saw it; never heard of it: I know not what it is.

*Eternal Wisdom.*—This is not surprising, for its strangeness and thy familiarity with creatures were the cause. But now open thy interior eyes and see who I am. It is I, the Eternal Wisdom, who, with the embrace of My eternal providence, have chosen thee in eternity for Myself alone. I have barred the way to thee as often as thou wouldst have parted company with Me, had I permitted thee. In all things thou didst ever meet with some obstacle and it is the sweet sign of My elect that I will needs have them for Myself.

*The Servant.*—Tender loving Wisdom! And is it Thou I have so long been seeking for? Is it Thou my spirit has so constantly struggled for? Alas, my God, why didst Thou not show Thyself to me long ago? Why hast Thou delayed so long? How many a weary way have I not wandered!

*Eternal Wisdom.*—Had I done so thou wouldst not have known My goodness so sensibly as now thou knowest it.

*The Servant.*—O unfathomable goodness! how very sweetly hast Thou not manifested Thyself to me! When I was not, Thou gavest me being. When I had separated from Thee, Thou didst not separate from me; when I wished to escape from Thee, Thou didst hold me sweetly captive. Yes, Thou Eternal Wisdom, if my heart might embrace Thee and consume all my days with Thee in love and praise, such would be its desire; for truly that man is blest whom Thou dost anticipate so lovingly that Thou lettest him have nowhere true rest, till he seeks his rest in Thee alone. O Wisdom Elect! since in Thee I have found Him whom my soul loveth, despise not Thy poor creature. See how dumb my heart is to all the world in joy and sorrow. Lord, is my heart always to be dumb towards Thee? O give my wretched soul leave, my dearest Lord, to speak a word with Thee, for my heart is too full to contain itself any longer; neither has it anyone in all this world to whom it can unburden itself, except to Thee, my elected Lord, Father, and Brother. Lord, Thou alone knowest the nature of a love-overflowing heart, and knowest that no one can love what he cannot in any way know. Therefore, since I am now to love Thee alone, give me to know Thee entirely, so that I may be also able to love Thee entirely.

*Eternal Wisdom.*—The highest emanation of all beings, taken in their natural order, is through the noblest beings to the lowest, but their refluence to their origin is through the lowest to the highest. Therefore, if thou art wishful to behold Me in My uncreated Divinity thou must learn how to know and love Me here in My suffering humanity for this is the speediest way to eternal salvation.

*The Servant.*—Then let me remind Thee to-day, Lord, of Thy unfathomable love, when Thou didst incline Thyself from Thy lofty throne, from the royal seat of the fatherly heart, in misery and disgrace for three-and-thirty years, and didst show the love which Thou hast for me and all mankind, principally in the most bitter passion of Thy cruel death: Lord, be Thou reminded of this, that Thou mayest manifest Thyself spiritually to my soul, in that most sweet and lovely form to which Thy immeasurable love did bring Thee.

*Eternal Wisdom.*—The more mangled, the more deathly I am for love, the more lovely am I to a well-regulated mind. My unfathomable love shows itself in the great bitterness of My passion, like the sun in its brightness, like the fair rose in its perfume, like the strong fire in its glowing heat. Therefore, hear with devotion how cruelly I suffered for thee.

## 2
## WHAT HAPPENED BEFORE THE CRUCIFIXION

*A*fter the Last Supper, when on the Mount of Olives, I gave Myself up to the pangs of cruel death, and when I felt that he was present before Me, I was bathed in a bloody sweat, because of the anguish of My tender Heart, and the agony of My whole bodily nature. I was ignominiously betrayed, taken prisoner like an enemy, rigorously bound, and led miserable away. After this I was impiously maltreated with blows, with spittle, with blindfolding, accused before Caiphas, and pronounced worthy of death. Unspeakable sorrows of heart were then seen in My dear Mother, from the first sight she had of My distress till I was hung upon the cross. I was shamefully presented before Pilate, falsely denounced, and sentenced to die. They stood over against Me with terrible eyes like fierce giants, and I stood before them like a meek lamb. I, the Eternal Wisdom, was mocked as a fool in a white garment before Herod, My fair body was rent and torn without mercy by the rude stripes of whips, My lovely countenance was drenched in spittle and blood, and in this condition I was condemned, and miserable and shamefully led forth with My cross to death. They shouted after Me very furiously, so that: Crucify, crucify the miscreant! resounded to the skies.

*The Servant.*—Alas! Lord, the beginning is indeed so bitter, how will it end? If I were to see a wild beast so abused I should hardly be able to bear it. With what reason, then, must not Thy Passion pierce my heart and soul! But, Lord, this is a great marvel to my heart; I would needs seek Thy divinity, and Thou showest me Thy humanity; I would needs seek Thy sweetness, and Thou settest before me Thy bitterness; I would needs conquer, Thou teachest me to fight. Lord, what dost Thou mean?

*Eternal Wisdom.*—No one can attain divine exaltation or singular sweetness except by passing through the image of My human abasement and bitterness. The higher one climbs without passing through My humanity, the deeper one falls. My humanity is the way one must go, My Passion the gate through which one must penetrate, to arrive at that which thou seekest. Therefore, lay aside thy faint-heartedness, and enter with Me the lists of knightly resolve: for, indeed, softness beseems not the servant when his master stands ready in warlike boldness. I will put thee on My coat of mail, for My entire Passion must thou suffer over again according to thy strength. Make up thy mind to a daring encounter, for thy heart, before thou shalt subdue thy nature, must often die, and thou must sweat the bloody sweat of anguish because of many a painful suffering under which I mean to prepare thee for Myself; for with red blossoms will I manure thy spice garden. Contrary to old custom, must thou be made prisoner and bound; thou wilt often be secretly calumniated and publicly defamed by My adversaries; many a false judgment will people pass on thee; My torments must thou then diligently carry in thy heart with a motherly heartfelt love. Thou wilt obtain many a severe judge of thy godly life; so also will thy godly ways be often mocked as folly by human ways; thy undisciplined body will be scourged with a hard and severe life; thou wilt be scoffingly crowned with persecution of thy holy life; after this, if only thou shalt issue forth from thy own will and deny thyself, and shalt stand as wholly disengaged from all creatures in the things which might lead thee astray in thy eternal salvation, even as a dying man when he departs hence, and has nothing more to do with this world—if only thou shalt do this, then wilt thou be led forth with Me on the miserable way of the cross.

*The Servant.*—Woe is me, Lord, but this is a dreary pastime! My whole nature rebels against these words. Lord, how shall I ever endure it all? Gentle Lord, one thing I must say: couldst Thou not have found out some other way, in Thy eternal wisdom, to save me and show Thy love for me, some way which would have exempted Thee from Thy great sufferings, and me from their bitter participation? How very wonderful do Thy judgments appear!

*Eternal Wisdom.*—The bottomless abyss of My hidden mysteries (in which I order everything according to My eternal providence), let no one explore, for no one can fathom it. And yet, in this abyss, what thou askest about and many things besides are possible, which yet never happen. However, know this much, that, in the order in which emanated beings now are, a more acceptable or more pleasing way could not be. The Lord of nature knows well what He can do in nature. He knows what is best suited to every creature, and He operates accordingly. How should man better know the hidden things of God than in His assumed Humanity? How might he, who has forfeited all joy through irregular lusts, be rendered susceptible of regular and eternal joy? How would it be possible to follow the unpracticed way of a hard and despised life, unless it had been followed by God Himself? If thou didst lie under sentence of death, how could He, who should suffer the fatal penalty in thy stead, better prove His fidelity and love towards thee, or better excite thee to love Him in return? Him, therefore, whom My unfathomable love, My unspeakable mercy, and My bright divinity, My most affable humanity, brotherly truth, espousing friendship, cannot move to ardent love, what else shall soften his stony heart? Ask the fair array of all created beings if ever I could have maintained My justice, evinced My fathomless mercy, ennobled human nature, poured out My goodness, reconciled heaven and earth, in a way more efficacious than by My bitter death?

*The Servant.*—Lord, truly, I begin to perceive that it is even so, and he whom want of understanding has not blinded, and who well considers the subject, must confess it to Thee, and extol the beautiful ways of Thy love above all ways. But still to follow Thee is very painful to a slothful body.

*Eternal Wisdom.*—Be not terrified at the following of My Passion. For he whose interior is so possessed by God that suffering is easy to him has no cause to complain. No one enjoys Me more in

My singular sweetness than he who stands with Me in harsh bitterness. No one complains so much of the bitterness of the husks as he to whom the interior sweetness of the kernel is unknown. For him who has a good second the fight is half won.

*The Servant.*—Lord, Thy comforting words have given me such heart, that, methinks, I am able to do and suffer all things in Thee. Therefore, I desire that Thou wouldst unlock for me the entire treasure of Thy Passion, and tell me still more about it.

## 3
# HOW IT WAS WITH HIM ON THE CROSS ACCORDING TO THE EXTERIOR MAN

*Eternal Wisdom.*—When I was suspended on the lofty tree of the cross because of My unfathomable love to thee and all mankind, My whole frame was very grievously distorted, My bright eyes were extinguished and turned in My head; My divine ears were filled with scoffing and blasphemy; My delicate nostrils were wounded with foul smells; My sweet mouth was tormented with bitter drink; and My tender feeling with hard blows. The whole earth was not able to afford Me any rest, for My feeble head was bowed down with pain and distress, My fair throat was unnaturally distended, My pure countenance polluted with spittle, My beautiful complexion faded. Lo! My comely figure withered entirely away, as though I were an outcast leper, and had never been the fair and Eternal Wisdom.

*The Servant.*—O Thou most gracious mirror of all graces, in which the heavenly spirits regale and feed their eyes, would that I had before me Thy delicious countenance in its deathly aspect until I had well steeped it in the tears of my heart; would that I might behold again and again those beautiful eyes, those bright cheeks, that tender mouth, all ghastly and dead, till I had fully relieved my heart in fervent lamentation over my Love. Alas! sweet Lord, Thy Passion affects so deeply the hearts of some people that they are able to lament over Thee with the greatest fervour, and weep for Thee from their very hearts. O God, could I, and might I, now represent all devout hearts with my lamentation, might I shed the tears of all eyes, and utter the doleful words of all tongues, then would I show Thee to-day how near to my heart Thy woeful Passion lies.

*Eternal Wisdom.*—No one can better show how deeply his heart is affected by My Passion than he who endures it with Me in the practice of good works. To Me, a free heart, unconcerned about perishable love, and ever intent on following the main thing according to the type of My contemplated Passion, is more agreeable than if thou didst always bewail Me, and didst shed as many tears from weeping over My torments as there ever rained drops of water from the sky; for the following of Me was the cause in which I suffered bitter death, although tears are also pleasing and agreeable to Me.

*The Servant.*—O sweet Lord, since then an affectionate following of Thy meek life and voluntary Passion is so agreeable to Thee, I will in future be more assiduous in a voluntary following than in a weeping sorrow. But, as I ought to have both, according to Thy words, teach me how I shall resemble Thee in both.

*Eternal Wisdom.*—Renounce thy pleasure in dissolute sights and voluptuous words; let that savour sweetly of love, and be grateful to thee, which before was repugnant to thee; thou shouldst seek all thy rest in Me, shouldst willingly suffer wrong from others, desire contempt, mortify thy passions, and die to all thy lusts. Such is the first lesson in the school of wisdom, which is to be read in the open, distended book of My crucified body. And consider and see, whether, if any one in all this world were to do his utmost, he could yet be to Me what I am to him?

## 4
# HOW VERY FAITHFUL HIS PASSION WAS

*The Servant.*—Lord, if I forget Thy worth, Thy gifts, Thy benefits, and all things, still *one* thing moves me and goes to my very heart; this is, when I well reflect not only on the way of our salvation, but also on its unfathomably faithful way. Dear Lord, many a one so bestows a gift on another, that his love and faith are better known by his way than by his gift. A small gift in a faithful way is often better than a great one without this way. Now, Lord, not only is Thy gift so great, but also the way of it, methinks, is so unfathomably faithful. Thou didst not only suffer death for me, but Thou didst also seek whatever is deepest in love, whatever is most intimate and hidden, in which suffering can or may be experienced. Thou didst really do as though Thou hadst said: Behold all hearts, if ever a heart was so full of love; look on all my limbs; the noblest limb I have is my heart; my very heart have I permitted to be pierced through, to be slain and consumed, and bruised into small pieces, that nothing in me or upon me might remain unbestowed, so that ye might know my love. Alas! Lord, how was it in Thy mind, or what were Thy thoughts? Might one not indeed learn something farther on this head?

*Eternal Wisdom.*—Never was there a thirsty mouth that longed so ardently for the cool fountain, nor a dying man for the pleasant days of life, as I longed to help all sinners and to render Myself beloved of them. Sooner couldst thou recall the days that are gone, sooner couldst thou make green all withered flowers, and gather up every drop of rain, than possess the power to measure the love which I bear to thee and all mankind. And, therefore, was I so covered with marks of love that one could not have placed the small point of a needle on any spot of My lacerated body that had not its particular love-mark. Consider that My right hand was nailed through; My right arm stretched out; My left very grievously distended; My right foot perforated; My left cruelly transfixed; that I hung fainting, and in great distress of My divine limbs; all My delicate members were immovably fastened to the hard bed of the cross. My hot blood, because of My anguish, burst forth in many a wild gush, which overflowed My expiring body, so that it was a most piteous sight to see. Behold a lamentable thing! My young, My fair and blooming body began to fade, to wither and pine away, My weary and tender back had a hard pillow on the rough cross, My heavy body gave way, My whole frame was gashed with wounds, and like one great sore, and all this My loving heart willingly endured.

## 5
## HOW THE SOUL ATTAINS HEARTY REPENTANCE AND GENTLE PARDON UNDER THE CROSS

*The Servant.*—Now then, cheer up thou soul of mine! Collect thyself entirely from all exterior things into the calm silence of thy interior, that so thou mayest break away, and wander at large, and run wild in the rugged wilderness of an unfathomable sorrow of heart, up to the high rock of misery, now contemplated; and mayest cry aloud from the depths of thy sad and languishing heart, till it resound over hill and valley throughout the sky, and pierce even to heaven before all the heavenly host; and speak with thy lamentable voice thus: Alas, ye living rocks, ye savage beasts, ye sunny meads! who will give me the burning fire of my full heart, and the scalding water of my sorrowful tears, to wake you up, that ye may help me to bewail the unfathomable heartrending woe which my poor heart so secretly suffers? Me had my heavenly Father adorned above all living creatures, and elected to be His own tender and blessed spouse. And lo, I have fled from Him! Woe is me! I have lost the beloved of my choice, my only one! Woe on my wretched heart! forever woe! What have I done, what have I lost! I have fled from myself, all the host of heaven, all that could give me joy and delight, have fled from me! I sit forsaken, for my false lovers were deceivers. O misery and death! How falsely and miserably have ye not forsaken me, how despoiled me of all the good with which my only love had arrayed me! Alas honour! alas joy! alas all consolation! how am I utterly robbed of you! Whither shall I turn myself? The entire world has forsaken me, because I have forsaken my only love. Wretched me! when I did so what a lamentable hour it was! Behold in me a late daisy, behold in me a sloe thorn, all ye red roses, ye white lilies! take notice how very quickly that flower withers, fades, and dies, which this world gathers! For I must always thus living, die; thus blooming, fade; thus youthful, grow old; thus healthy, sicken. And yet, tender Lord, all that I suffer is of small account compared to my having made wroth Thy fatherly countenance; for this is to me a hell and a grief above all grief. Alas, that Thou shouldst have been so graciously kind, that

Thou shouldst have warned me so tenderly, and drawn me so affectionately, and that I should have so utterly despised it all! O heart of man! what canst thou not endure! As hard as steel must thou be not to burst utterly with woe. True, I was once called His beloved spouse: woe is me! I am not now worthy to be called His poor handmaid. Nevermore, for bitter shame, may I raise my eyes. Henceforth in joy and sorrow my mouth to Him must be dumb. O how narrow for me is this wide world! O God, were I but in a wild forest, where no one might hear or see me, but where I could cry aloud to my heart's desire, to the relief of my poor heart; for other consolation I have none! O sin, to what a pass has thou brought me! Woe to thee, thou false world! woe to him that serves thee! How hast thou rewarded me, seeing that I am a burthen to myself and thee, and ever must be. Hail, all hail to you, ye rich queens! ye rich souls, who, by the misfortunes of others, have become wise; who have continued in your first innocence of body and mind; how unwittingly blessed ye are! O pure conscience! O free and single heart! how ignorant are ye of the state of a heart oppressed and sorrowful through sin! Ah me, poor spouse, how happy was I with my Beloved, and how little did I know it! Who will give me the breadth of the heavens for parchment, the depth of the sea for ink, leaves and grass for pens, that I may write fully out my desolation of soul, and the irreparable calamity which my woeful separation from my Beloved has brought upon me! Alas that ever I was born! What is left but for me to cast myself into the abyss of despair?

*Eternal Wisdom.*—Thou must not despair. Did I not come into the world for the sake of thee and all sinners, that I might lead thee back to My Father in such beauty, brightness, and purity, as otherwise thou never couldst have acquired?

*The Servant.*—O what is that which sounds so sweetly in a dead and outcast soul?

*Eternal Wisdom.*—Dost thou not know Me? What! art thou fallen so low, or hast thou lost thy senses, because of thy great trouble, my tender child? And yet it is I, the all-merciful Wisdom, I Who have opened wide the abyss of infinite mercy, which is, however, hidden from all the saints, to receive thee and all penitent hearts. It is I, the sweet Eternal Wisdom, who became wretched and poor that I might guide thee back again to thy dignity. It is I, Who suffered bitter death that I might bring thee again to life. Lo, here I am, pale, bloody, affectionate, as when suspended between thee and the severe judgment of My Father, on the lofty gibbet of the cross. It is I, thy brother. Behold, it is I, thy bridegroom! Everything that thou ever didst against Me will I wholly forget, as though it had never happened, provided only that thou return to Me, and never quit Me more. Wash thyself in My precious blood, lift up thy head, open thy eyes, and be of good cheer. Receive as a token of entire peace and complete expiation My wedding ring on thy hand, receive thy first robe, shoes on thy feet, and the fond name of My bride for ever! Lo, I have garnered thee up with such bitter toil! Therefore, if the whole world were a consuming fire, and there lay in the midst of it a handful of flax, it would not, from its very nature, be so susceptible of the burning flame as the abyss of My mercy is ready to pardon a repentant sinner, and blot out his sins.

*The Servant.*—O my Father! O my Brother! O all that can ravish my heart! And wilt Thou still be gracious to my offending soul? O what goodness, what unfathomable compassion! For this will I fall prostrate at Thy feet, O heavenly Father! and thank Thee from the bottom of my heart, and beg of Thee to look on Thy only-begotten Son, whom, out of love Thou gavest to bitter death, and to forget my grievous misdeeds. Remember, heavenly Father, how Thou didst swear of old to Noah, and didst say: I will stretch My bow in the sky; I will look upon it, and it shall be a sign of reconciliation between Me and the earth. O look now upon it, tender Father, how cruelly stretched out it is, so that its bones and ribs can be numbered; look how red, how green, how yellow, love has made it! Look, O heavenly Father, through the hands, the arms, and the feet, so woefully distended, of Thy tender and only-begotten Son. Look at His beautiful body, all rose colour with wounds, and forget Thy anger against me. Remember that Thou art only called the Lord of Mercy, the Father of Mercy, because Thou forgivest. Such is Thy name. To whom did Thou give Thy best-beloved Son? To sinners. Lord, he is MINE! Lord, he is ours! This very day will I enclose myself with His bare extended arms in a loving embrace in the bottom of my heart and soul, and living or dead will never more be separated from Him. Therefore, do Him honour to-day in me, and graciously forget that wherein I may have angered Thee. For, methinks it were easier for me to suffer death than ever to anger Thee, my heavenly Father, again. Neither afflictions nor oppressions, neither hell nor purgatory, are such causes of lamentation to my heart, as that I ever should have angered and dishonoured Thee, my Creator, my Lord, my God, my Saviour, the joy and delight of my heart. Oh, if for this I could give voice to my grief of soul, through all the heavens, till my heart should burst into a thousand pieces, how gladly would I do it! And the more entirely Thou forgivest my evil deeds, so much the greater is my sorrow of heart at having been so ungrateful in return for thy great goodness. And Thou, my only consolation, Thou my tender elected one, Eternal Wisdom! how can I ever make Thee a complete and proper return of thanks for having at so dear a rate healed and reconciled with Thy pangs and wounds the breach which all created beings could not have made good? And, therefore, my eternal joy, teach me how to bear Thy wounds and love-marks on my entire body, and how to have them at all times in my keeping, so that all this world, and all the heavenly host, may see that I am grateful for the infinite good which, out of Thy unfathomable goodness alone, Thou hast bestowed on my lost soul.

*Eternal Wisdom.*—Thou shouldst give thyself and all that is thine to Me cheerfully, and never take them back. All that is not of absolute necessity to thee shouldst thou leave untouched; then will thy hands be truly nailed to My cross. Thou shouldst cheerfully set about good works and persevere in them; then will thy left foot be made fast. Thy inconstant mind and wandering thoughts shouldst thou make constant and collected in Me; and thus thy right foot will be nailed to My cross. Thy mental and bodily powers must not seek rest in lukewarmness; in the likeness of My arms they should be stretched out in My service. Thy sickly body must often, in honour of my dislocated bones, be wearied out in spiritual exercises, and rendered incapable of fulfilling its own desires. Many an unknown suffering must strain thee to Me on the narrow bed of the cross, by which thou wilt become lovely like Me, and of the colour of blood. The withering away of thy nature must make Me blooming again; thy spontaneous hardships must be to My weary back as a bed; thy resolute resistance to sin must relieve My spirit; thy devout heart must soften My pains, and thy high flaming heart must kindle My fervid heart.

*The Servant.*—Now, then, fulfill Thou my good wishes, according to Thy highest praise, and according to Thy very best will; for indeed Thy yoke is sweet, and Thy burthen light: this do all those know who have experienced it, and who were once overladen with the heavy load of sin.

## 6
# HOW DECEITFUL THE LOVE OF THIS WORLD IS, AND HOW AMIABLE GOD IS

*The Servant.*—Sweetest God, if I leave Thee but a little I am like a young roe which has strayed from its dam, and is pursued by the hunter, and runs wildly about, until it escapes back to its cover. Lord, I flee, I run to Thee with ardent desire, like a stag to the living waters. Lord, one little hour without Thee is a whole year; to be estranged one day from Thee is as much as a thousand years to a loving heart. Therefore, Thou branch of salvation, Thou bush of May, Thou red blooming rose-tree, open and spread out the green branches of Thy divine nature. Lord, Thy countenance is so full of graciousness, Thy mouth so full of living words, Thy whole carriage such a pure mirror of all discipline and meekness! O Thou aspect of graciousness to all the saints, how very blessed is he who is found worthy of Thy sweet espousals!

*Eternal Wisdom,*—Many are called to them, but few are chosen.

*The Servant.*—Gentle Lord, either they have broken with Thee, or Thou with them.

*Eternal Wisdom.*—Lift up, therefore, thy eyes, and behold this vision.

*The Servant* lifted up his eyes and was terrified, and, with a deep sigh, said: Woe to me, dear Lord, that ever I was born! Do I see aright, or is it only a dream? I saw Thee before in such richness of beauty, and such tenderness of love; now I see nothing but a poor, outcast, miserable pilgrim who stands wretchedly leaning on his staff before an old decayed city. The trenches are in ruins, the walls falling down, only that, here and there, the high tops of the old timber work still project aloft; and in the city is a great multitude of people; among them are many that look like wild beasts in a human form: and the miserable pilgrim goes wandering about to see if any one will take him by the hand. Alas! I behold the multitude drive him with insult away, and hardly look at him, because of the things about which they are busy. And yet some, but only a very few, offer to give him their hands; this the other wild beasts come and prevent. Now I hear the miserable pilgrim begin to sigh woefully, and cry aloud: O heaven and earth have pity on me—me who have garnered up this city with such bitter toil, and who am so badly welcomed in it, while those who have spent no labour upon it are yet so kindly received!

Lord, such is what has been shown me in the vision. O Thou eternal God, what does it mean? Am I right or wrong?

*Eternal Wisdom.*—This vision is a vision of pure truth. Hearken to a lamentable thing; O let it touch thy heart with pity! I am the miserable pilgrim whom thou didst see. At one time I was in great honour in that city, but now I am brought down to great misery and driven out.

*The Servant.*—Dearest Lord! what is this city, what are the people in it?

*Eternal Wisdom.*—This decayed city is an image of that spiritual life in which I was once so worthily served. And while they were living in it so holily and securely, it begins in many places to fall very much to ruin; the trenches begin to decay, and the walls to crack, that is to say, devout obedience, voluntary poverty, secluded purity in holy simplicity, begin to disappear, and, at last, to such a degree that nothing is to be seen standing, except the high timber work of mere exterior observance. As to the great multitude, the beasts in human form, they are worldly hearts under spiritual disguises, who, in the vain pursuit of transitory things, drive Me out of their souls. That a few should, nevertheless, offer to give Me their hands, but are hindered by the rest, signifies that some men of good intentions and devout feelings are perverted by the speech and evil example of others. The staff on which thou didst see Me stand leaning, is the cross of My bitter passion, with which I admonish them at all times to think on My sufferings, and to turn, with the love of their hearts to Me alone. But the cry of misery thou didst hear is My death which even here begins to cry aloud, and ever cries aloud, because of those in whom neither My unfathomable love nor My bitter death is able to do so much as to expel the worm of sinful thoughts from their hearts.

*The Servant.*—O Lord, how it cuts through my very heart and soul to think Thou art so lovable, and yet, in spite of all Thy advances, art in many hearts so utterly despised. Ah! tender Lord, what will Thy advances be to those who, though they see Thee in the miserable shape in which Thou art rejected by the multitude, yet stretch out their hands to Thee with sincere faith and love?

*Eternal Wisdom.*—Those who for My sake give up perishable affections, and receive Me with sincere faith and love, and remain constant to the end, will I espouse with My divine love and sweetness, and will give them My hand in death, and exalt them on the throne of My glory before the whole court of heaven.

*The Servant.*—Lord, there be many who think they will still love Thee without giving up perishable love. Lord, they will needs be very dear to Thee, and yet will not the less indulge in temporal love.

*Eternal Wisdom.*—It is as impossible as to compress the heavens together and enclose them in a nut shell. Such persons array themselves in fair words, they build upon the wind, and construct upon the rainbow. How may the eternal abide with the temporal, when even one temporal thing neither can nor will endure another? He but deceives himself who thinks he can lodge the King of kings in a common inn, or thrust Him into the mean dwelling of a servant. In entire seclusion from all creatures must he keep himself who is desirous of receiving his guest as he ought.

*The Servant.*—Alas, sweet Lord, how completely bewitched must they all be not to see this!

*Eternal Wisdom.*—They stand in deep blindness. They endure many a hard struggle for pleasures which yet neither fix their attachment nor afford them full gratification. Before they obtain one joy they meet with ten sorrows, and the more they pursue their lusts the more are these upbraided with being insufficient. Lo! godless hearts must needs be at all times in fear and trembling. Even the fleeting pleasure they obtain proves very harsh to them, for they procure it with much toil, they enjoy it in great anxiety, and lose it with much bitterness. The world is full of untruth, falsehood, and inconstancy; when profit is at an end, friendship is at an end, and to speak shortly, neither true love, nor entire joy, nor constant peace of mind, was ever obtained by any heart from creatures.

*The Servant.*—Alas! dear Lord, what a lamentable thing it is, that so many a noble soul, so many a languishing heart, so many an image formed after God in such beauty and sweetness, that in Thy espousals ought to be queens and empresses, powerful in heaven and on earth, should so foolishly go astray and degrade themselves! Oh, wonder of wonders! to think that of their own accord they should be lost! since, according to Thy words of truth, the fell separation of the soul from the body were better for them than that Thou, the Life Eternal, shouldest have to separate from their souls where Thou findest no dwelling-place. Oh, ye dull fools, behold how your great ruin prospers, how your great loss increases, how you allow the precious, the fair, the delightsome moments to pass away, which ye may hardly or indeed never again possess, and how gaily you carry yourselves the while, as though it concerned you not! Alas! Thou gentle

Wisdom, did they but know it and feel it surely they would desist.

*Eternal Wisdom.*—Listen to a wonderful and lamentable thing. They know it and feel it at all hours, and yet do not desist; they know it and yet will not know it; they beautify it, like unsound argument, with dazzling brightness, which yet is unlike the naked truth, as so many of them at last, when it is too late, will have to feel.

*The Servant.*—Alas! tender Wisdom, how senseless they are, or what does it mean?

*Eternal Wisdom.*—Here will they needs escape calamity and suffering, and yet fall into the midst of it; and as they will not endure the eternal good and My sweet yoke, they will be overwhelmed by the inevitable doom of My severe justice with many a heavy burthen. They fear the frost, and fall into the snow.

*The Servant.*—Alas! tender and merciful Wisdom, remember that, without being strengthened by Thee, no one can accomplish anything. I see no other help for them than to raise their eyes to Thee, and to fall at Thy feet with bitter, heart-felt tears, entreating that Thou wouldst vouchsafe to enlighten them, and free them from the bonds with which they are made fast.

*Eternal Wisdom.*—I am at all times ready to help them, if only they be ready. I do not turn away from them.

*The Servant.*—Lord, it is painful for love to separate from love.

*Eternal Wisdom.*—Very true, if I could not and would not lovingly make good all love in hearts of love.

*The Servant.*—O Lord, it is impossible to leave off old custom.

*Eternal Wisdom.*—But it will be yet more impossible to endure future torments.

*The Servant.*—They are perhaps so well regulated in themselves that it does them no injury.

*Eternal Wisdom.*—I was the best regulated of men, and yet the most self-mortified. How may that be regulated which, from its very nature, corrupts the heart, confuses the mind, perverts discipline, draws off the heart from all fervour, and robs it of its peace? It breaks open the gates, behind which godly living lies hidden, that is, the five senses. It casts forth sobriety and introduces audaciousness, the loss of grace, estrangement from God, interior tepidity, and exterior sloth.

*The Servant.*—Lord, they do not think they are hindered so much, if only what they love have the appearance of a spiritual life.

*Eternal Wisdom.*—A clear-seeing eye may just as easily be blinded by white meal as by pale ashes. Behold, was ever any person's presence so harmless as Mine among My disciples? No unprofitable words fell from us, among us there was no extravagant demeanour, no beginning loftily in the spirit, and sinking down in the depth of endless words; there was nothing but real earnestness and entire truth without any deceit. And yet, My bodily presence had to be withdrawn from them before they became susceptible of My spirit. What a hindrance, then, must not a merely human presence prove! Before they are influenced to good by one person, they are seduced by a thousand; before they are reformed in one point by good precept, they are often led astray by bad example; and, to speak briefly, as the sharp frost in May nips the blossoms and scatters them abroad, so the love of perishable things blights godly seriousness and religious discipline. If thou hast still a doubt respecting it, look around thee into the beautiful, fruitful vineyards which formerly were so delightful in their first bloom, how utterly withered and ruined they are, so that they contain few traces more of fervent seriousness and great devotion. Now, this produces an irreparable injury, for it has become a thing of habit, a spiritual decorum, which, secretly, is so destructive of all spiritual salvation. It is all the more pernicious as it appears innocent. How many a precious spice-garden is there, which, adorned with delightful gifts, was a heavenly paradise, where God was well pleased to dwell, which, now, by reason of perishable love, has become a garden of wild weeds; where lilies and roses formerly grew, now stands thorns, nettles, and briars, and where angels were used to dwell, swine now root up the soil. Woe betide the hour, when all lost time, when all good works neglected, shall be reckoned up, when every idle word spoken, thought written, whether in secret or in public, shall be read out before God and the whole world, and its meaning, without disguise, be understood!

*The Servant.*—Alas! Lord these words are so sharp that indeed it must be a stony heart that is not moved by them. Ah, my Lord, some hearts there are, of so tender a nature, that they are much sooner attracted by love than fear, and as Thou, the Lord of nature, art not a destroyer but a fulfiller of nature, O, therefore, most kind and gracious Lord, put an end to this sad discourse, and tell me how Thou art a Mother of beautiful love, and how sweet Thy love is.

# 7
# HOW LOVELY GOD IS

*The Servant.*—Lord, let me reflect on that divine passage, where Thou speakest of Thyself in the Book of Wisdom: "Come over to Me, all ye that desire Me, and be filled with My fruits. I am the Mother of fair love; My spirit is sweet above honey and the honeycomb. Wine and music rejoice the heart, but the love of wisdom is above them both.*

Ah, Lord! Thou canst show Thyself so lovely and so tender, that all hearts must needs languish for Thee and endure, for Thy sake, all the misery of tender desire; Thy words of love flow so sweetly out of Thy sweet mouth, and so powerfully affect many hearts in their days of youthful

---
* Ecclesiasticus xxiv. 24, 26, 27; xl. 20

bloom, that perishable love is wholly extinguished in them. O my dear Lord, this it is for which my soul sighs, this it is which makes my spirit sad, this it is about which I would gladly hear Thee speak. Now, then, my only elected Comforter, speak one little word to my soul, to Thy poor handmaid; for, lo! I am fallen softly asleep beneath Thy shadow, and my heart watcheth.

*Eternal Wisdom.*—Listen, then, my son, and see, incline to Me thy ears, enter wholly into thy interior, and forget thyself and all things. I am in Myself the incomprehensible good, which always was and always is, which never was and never will be uttered. I may indeed give Myself to men's hearts to be felt by them, but no tongue can truly express Me in words. And yet, when I, the Supernatural, immutable good, present Myself to every creature according to its capacity to be susceptible of Me, I bind the sun's splendour, as it were, in a cloth, and give thee spiritual perceptions of Me and of My sweet love in bodily words thus: I set Myself tenderly before the eyes of thy heart; now adorn and clothe thou Me in spiritual perceptions and represent Me as delicate and as comely as thy very heart could wish, and bestow on Me all those things that can move the heart to especial love and entire delight of soul. Lo! all and everything that thou and all men can possibly imagine of form, of elegance, and grace, is in Me far more ravishing than any one can express, and in words like these do I choose to make Myself known. Now, listen further: I am of high birth, of noble race; I am the Eternal Word of the Fatherly Heart, in which, according to the love-abounding abyss of My natural Sonship in His sole paternity, I possess a gratefulness before His tender eyes in the sweet and bright-flaming love of the Holy Ghost. I am the throne of delight, I am the crown of salvation, My eyes are so clear, My mouth so tender, My cheeks so radiant and blooming, and all My figure so fair and ravishing, yea, and so delicately formed, that if a man were to lie in a glowing furnace till the day of judgment, only to have one single glance at My beauty, he would not deserve it. See, I am so deliciously adorned in garments of light, I am so exquisitely set off with all the blooming colours of living flowers, that all May-blossoms, all the beautiful shrubs of all dewy fields, all the tender buds of the sunny meads, are but as rough thistles compared to My adornment.

>    In the Godhead I play the
>       game of bliss,
>    Such joy the angels find in
>       this,

> That unto them a thousand years
> But as one little hour appears.

All the heavenly host follow Me entranced by new wonders, and behold Me; their eyes are fixed on Mine; their hearts are inclined to Me, their minds bent on Me without intermission. Happy is he who, in joyous security, shall take Me by My beautiful hand, and join in My sweet diversions, and dance for ever the dance of joy amid the ravishing delights of the kingdom of heaven! One little word there spoken by My sweet mouth will far surpass the singing of all angels, the music of all harps, the harmony of all sweet strings. My faithfulness is so made to be loved, so lovely am I to be embraced, and so tender for pure languishing souls to kiss, that all hearts ought to break for My possession. I am condescending and full of sympathy and always present to the pure soul. I abide with her in secret, at table, in bed, in the streets, in the fields. Turn Myself whichever way I will, in Me there is nothing that can displease, in Me is everything that can delight the utmost wishes of thy heart and desires of the soul. Lo! I am a good so pure, that he who in his day only gets one drop of Me regards all the pleasures and delights of this world as nothing but bitterness; all its possessions and honours as worthless, and only fit to be cast away; My beloved ones are encompassed by My love, and are absorbed into the One Thing alone without imaged love and without spoken words, and are taken and infused into that good out of which they flowed. My love can also relieve regenerate hearts from the heavy load of sin, and can give a free, pure, and gentle heart, and create a clean conscience. Tell Me, what is there in all this world able to outweigh this one thing? For he who gives his heart wholly to Me lives joyfully, dies securely, and obtains the kingdom of heaven here as well as hereafter.

Now, observe, I have assuredly given thee many words, and yet My beauty has been as little touched by them as the firmament by thy little finger, because no eye has ever seen My beauty, nor ear heard it, neither has it ever entered any heart. Still let what I have said to thee be as a device to show thee the difference between My sweet love and false, perishable love.

*The Servant.*—Ah! Thou tender, delicious, wild flower, Thou delight of the heart in the embracing arms of the pure loving soul, how familiar is all this to him who has even once really felt Thee; but how strange is it to that man who knows Thee not, whose heart and mind are still of the body! O, Thou most heart-felt incomprehensible good this is a precious hour, this is a sweet moment, in which I must open to Thee a secret wound which my heart still bears from Thy sweet love. Lord, plurality in love is like water in the fire. Lord, Thou knowest that real fervent love cannot bear duality. Alas! Thou only Lord of my heart and soul, my heart desires that Thou shouldst have a particular love for me, and that I should be particularly pleasing to Thy divine eyes. O Lord, Thou hast so many hearts that ardently love Thee, and are of much account with Thee. Alas! my sweet and tender Lord, how stands it with me in this matter?

*Eternal Wisdom.*—My love is of that sort which is not diminished in unity, nor confounded in multiplicity. I am as entirely concerned and occupied with thee alone, with the thought how I may at all times love thee alone, and fulfill everything that appertains to thee, as though I were wholly disengaged from all other things.

*The Servant.*—O rare! O wonderful! whither am I borne, how am I gone astray! how is my soul utterly dissolved by the sweet friendly words of my beloved! Oh, turn away Thy bright eyes from me, for they have overcome me.* Wherever was there a heart so hard, a soul so lukewarm, so cold as, when it heard Thy sweet living words, so ex-

---

* Cant. vi. 5

ceedingly fiery as they are, was not fain to melt and kindle in Thy sweet love! O wonder of wonders! that he who thus sees Thee with the eyes of his soul, should not feel his very heart dissolve in love. How right blessed is he who bears the name of Thy Spouse, and is so! What sweet consolations and secret tokens of Thy love must not he eternally receive from Thee! O thou sweet virgin St. Agnes, thou fair wooer of Eternal Wisdom! how well couldst thou console thyself with thy dear Bridegroom, when thou didst say, "His blood has adorned my cheeks as with roses." O gentle Lord, that my soul were but worthy to be called Thy wooer! And were it indeed possible that all delights, all joy and love, that this world can afford, might be found united in one man, how gladly would I renounce him for the sake of that name! How blessed is that man, that ever he was born into the world, who is named Thy friend, and is so! Oh, if a man had even a thousand lives, he ought to stake them at once for the sake of acquiring Thy love. Oh, all ye friends of God, all ye heavenly host, and thou dear virgin St. Agnes, help me to pray to Him: for never did I rightly know what His love was. Alas! thou heart of mine, lay aside, put away all sloth, and see if, before thy death, thou mayest advance so far as to feel His sweet love. O thou tender beautiful Wisdom! O my elected one! What a truly right gracious love Thou canst be above all loves else in the world! How very different is Thy love and the love of creatures! How false is everything that appears lovely in this world and gives itself out to be something, as soon as one really begins to know it. Lord, wherever I might cast my eyes I always found something to disgust me; for, if it was a fair image, it was void of grace; if it was fair and lovely, it had not the true way; or if it had indeed this, still, I always found something either inwardly or outwardly, to which the entire inclination of my heart was secretly opposed. But Thou art beauty with infinite affability, Thou art grace in shape and form, the word with the way, nobility with virtue, riches with power, interior freedom and exterior brightness, and ONE thing Thou art which I have never found in time, namely, a power and faculty of perfectly satiating every wish and every ardent desire of a truly loving heart. The more one knows Thee, the more one loves Thee; the more acquainted one is with Thee, the more friendly one finds Thee. Ah me! what an unfathomable, entirely pure, good Thou art! See how deceived all those hearts are that fix their affections on anything else! Ah! ye false lovers, flee far from me, never come near me more. I have chosen for my heart that one only love in which my heart, my soul, my desire, and all my powers can alone be satiated with a love that never dissolves away. Oh Lord, could I but trace Thee on my heart! could I but melt Thee with characters of gold into the innermost core of my heart and soul, so that Thou mightest never be eradicated out of me! Oh, misery and desolation! that ever I should have troubled my heart with such things! What have I gained with all my lovers, but time lost, forfeited words, an empty hand, few good works, and a conscience burdened with infirmity? Slay me, rather, in Thy love, O Lord, for from Thy feet I will never more be separated.

*Eternal Wisdom.*—I go forth to meet those who seek Me, and I receive with affectionate joy such as desire My love. All that thou canst ever experience of My sweet love in time, is but as a little drop to the ocean of My love in eternity.

# 8
# AN EXPLANATION

**OF THREE THINGS WHICH MOST OF ALL MIGHT BE LIKELY TO BE REPUGNANT TO A LOVING HEART IN GOD.—ONE IS, HOW HE CAN APPEAR SO WRATHFUL AND YET BE SO GRACIOUS.**

*The Servant.*—Three things there are at which I marvel very much; one is, that Thou shouldst be beyond all measure so amiable Thyself, and yet so severe a judge of evil deeds. Lord, when I reflect on Thy severe justice, my heart with passionate voice exclaims: "Woe to all who persist in sin!" for did they but know the strict account of every single sin, which Thou wilt infallibly require, even from Thy very dearest friends, they would sooner pluck out their teeth and hair than ever provoke Thy anger! Woe is me! How very terrible is Thy angry countenance, how very intolerable Thy ungentle averted looks! So full of fire are Thy threatening words that they cut through heart and soul. Shield me, O Lord, from Thy wrathful countenance, and extend not Thy vengeance against me to the next world. Lo! when I only doubt, lest, because of my guilty deeds Thou mayest have turned Thy face angrily away from me, it is a thing so insupportable, that nothing in all this world is so bitter to me. Oh, my Lord and Father, how could my heart endure Thy angry countenance for ever! When I but seriously reflect on Thy countenance inflamed with anger, my soul is so horrified, all my strength is so shaken, that I can liken it to nothing else than to the heavens beginning to darken and grow black, to fire raging in the clouds, and to a mighty thunder rending them, so that the earth trembles, and fiery bolts dart down upon men. Lord, let no one confide in Thy silence, for verily Thy silence will soon be turned to dreadful thunder. Lord, the angry countenance of Thy Fatherly anger to that man who is fearful of provoking and losing Thee, is a hell above all hells. I will say nothing of that furious countenance of Thine which the wicked at the last day will have to behold in bitterness of heart. Woe, everlasting woe to those who shall have to expect so great a calamity!

Lord, all this is a profound mystery to my heart, and yet Thou sayest that Thou art so gracious and so good.

*Eternal Wisdom.*—I am the immutable good, and subsist the same and am the same. But that I do not appear the same, arises from the difference of those who view Me differently, according as they are with or without sin. I am tender and loving in My nature, and yet a terrible judge of evil deeds. I require from My friends childlike awe, and confiding love, in order that awe may restrain them from sin, and love unite them to Me in faith.

## 9
## THE SECOND THING.

**Why God, After Rejoicing The Heart, Often Withdraws Himself From His Friends, By Which His True Presence is Made Known.**

*The Servant.*—Lord, all has been explained to my heart's satisfaction, except one thing. In truth, Lord, when a soul is quite exhausted with yearning after Thee and the sweet caresses of Thy presence, then, Lord, art Thou silent and sayest not a word. O Lord! ought not this to grieve my heart, that Thou, my tender Lord, Thou who art my only one love, and the sole desire of my heart, shouldst yet behave Thyself so strangely, and in such a way hold Thy peace?

*Eternal Wisdom.*—And yet do all creatures cry aloud to Me that it is I.

*The Servant.*—O dear Lord! that is not enough for a languishing soul.

*Eternal Wisdom.*—If every little word I utter is a little word of love to their hearts, and every word of the Sacred Scriptures written by Me is a sweet love-letter, as though I Myself had written it, ought this not to be enough for them?

*The Servant.*—O Lord, Thou knowest well that to a loving heart everything that is not its only love and its only consolation, is insufficient. Lord, Thou art so very intimate, choice, and fathomless a love; lo! if even all the tongues of all the angels were to address me, love unfathomable would still pursue and strive after Him alone whom it longs for. A loving soul would still take Thee for the kingdom of heaven, for surely Thou art her heaven. Alas! Lord, may I venture to say that Thou shouldst be a little more favourable to such poor affectionate hearts as pine and languish for Thee, as breathe out so many an unfathomable sigh to Thee, as look up so yearningly to Thee, crying aloud from their very hearts, Return to us, O Lord! and speaking and reasoning with themselves thus: "Have we cause to think we have angered Him, and that He will forsake us? Have we cause to think He will not give us His loving presence back again, so that we may affectionately embrace Him with the arms of our hearts, and press Him to our bosoms till all our sorrow vanish? Lord, all this Thou knowest and hearest, and yet Thou art silent!"

*Eternal Wisdom.*—I know it and see it with heart-felt eager joy. But now, since thy wonder is so great, answer Me a question. What is that which, of all things, gives the most delight to the highest of created spirits?

*The Servant.*—Lord, I would fain learn this from Thee, for such a question is too great for my understanding.

*Eternal Wisdom.*—Then I will tell Thee. Nothing tastes better to the very highest angel than, in all things, to do My will; so that if he knew that it would tend to My praise to root up nettles and other weeds it would be for him, of all things, the most desirable to perform.

*The Servant.*—Ah, Lord, how dost Thou strike home to me with this question! For surely Thy meaning is, that I ought to keep myself disengaged and serene in joy, and seek Thy praise alone, both in sorrow and delight.

*Eternal Wisdom.*—A desertion above all desertion is to be deserted in desertion.

*The Servant.*—Alas! Lord, but it is a very heavy woe.

*Eternal Wisdom.*—Where is virtue preserved except in adversity? Yet know that I often come and ask for admission into my house, and am denied. Often am I received like a poor pilgrim, and meanly entertained, and speedily driven out. I come even to My beloved, and fondly take up My abode with her, but this takes place so secretly that it is totally hidden from all men, except those only who live in entire seclusion, and perceive My ways, who are ever careful to correspond to My graces. For in virtue of My divinity, I am a perfectly pure essential spirit, and am spiritually received into pure spirits.

*The Servant.*—Gentle Lord, methinks Thou art altogether a hidden lover, therefore I desire Thou wouldst give me some signs of Thy true presence.

*Eternal Wisdom.*—In nothing canst thou discern My presence so well as in this, namely, when I hide and withdraw Myself from the soul, as not till then art thou capable of perceiving who I am or what thou art. I am the Eternal Good, without which no one has any good. When I, the Eternal Good, pour Myself out so graciously and lovingly, everything into which I enter is made good. By this goodness My presence is to be known even as is the sun by his brightness, who, in his substance, is yet not to be seen. If ever thou art sensible of Me, enter into thyself and learn to separate the roses from the thorns, and to choose out the flowers from the grass.

*The Servant.*—Lord, truly I seek and find in myself a great inequality. When my soul is deserted, she is like a sick person who can relish nothing; who is disgusted with everything; the body is languid, the spirits are dull; dryness within, and sadness without; all that I see and hear is then repugnant to me, and I know not how good it is, for I have lost all discrimination. I am then inclined to sin, weak in resisting my enemies, cold and lukewarm in all that is good; he who visits me finds an empty house, for the master, who gives wise counsel and makes all the family glad at heart, is not within. But, Lord, when in the midst of my soul the bright morning star rises, all my sorrow passes away, all my darkness is scattered, and laughing cheerfulness appears. Lord, then leaps my heart, then are my spirits gay, then rejoices my soul, then is it my marriage feast, while all that is in me or about me is turned to Thy praise. What before was hard, troublesome, and impossible, becomes easy and pleasant; fasting, watching, praying, self-denial, and every sort of rigour, are made sweet by Thy presence. Then do I acquire great assurance in many things, which, in my dereliction I had lost; my soul is then overflowed with clearness, truth, and sweetness, so that she forgets all her toil; my heart can sweetly meditate, my tongue loftily discourse, and whoever seeks high counsel from me touching his heart's desire finds it; for then I am as though I had overstepped the bounds of time and space, and stood in the ante-chamber of eternal salvation. Alas, Lord! who will grant that it might only be of longer duration, for behold, in a moment it is snatched away, and I am again stripped and forsaken. Sometimes I pursue it as if I had never gained it, till at last, after much sorrow and trouble of heart, it comes back. Lord! art Thou this thing, or am I it, or what is it?

*Eternal Wisdom.*—Thou art and hast of thyself nothing but imperfection; I am it, and this is the game of love.

*The Servant.*—But, Lord, what is the game of love?

*Eternal Wisdom.*—All the time that love is with love, love does not know how dear love is; but when love separates from love, then only does love feel how dear love was.

*The Servant.*—Lord! this is a dreary game. Alas, Lord! is inconstancy never cast aside in any one while time lasts?

*Eternal Wisdom.*—In very few persons, for constancy belongs to eternity.

*The Servant.*—Lord, who are these persons?

*Eternal Wisdom.*—The very purest of all, and in eternity the most like to God.

*The Servant.*—Lord, which are they?

*Eternal Wisdom.*—They are those persons who

have denied themselves in the most perfect manner.

*The Servant.*—Gentle Lord, teach me how, in my imperfection, I ought to behave in this manner.

*Eternal Wisdom.*—In good days thou oughtest to look at evil days, and in evil days not to forget good days; thus can neither elation injure thee in My company nor despondency in dereliction. If, in thy faintheartedness, thou canst not endure My absence with pleasure, wait for Me at least with patience, and seek Me diligently.

*The Servant.*—O Lord, long waiting is painful.

*Eternal Wisdom.*—He who will needs have love in time, must know how to bear weal and woe. It is not enough to devote to Me only a portion of the day. He who would enjoy God's intimacy, who would hear His mysterious words, and mark their secret meaning, ought always to keep within doors. Alas! how is it that thou always permittest thy eyes to wander so thoughtlessly around, when thou hast standing before thee the Blessed and Eternal Image of the Godhead which never for a moment turns away from thee? Why dost thou let thy ears escape from thee when I address thee so many a sweet word? How is it that thou so readily forgettest thyself when thou art so perfectly encompassed with the eternal good? What is it thy soul seeks in exterior things who carries within herself so secretly the kingdom of heaven?

*The Servant.*—What is the kingdom of heaven, O Lord, which is in the soul?

*Eternal Wisdom.*—It is righteousness, and peace, and joy in the Holy Ghost.

*The Servant.*—Lord, I understand from this discourse, that Thou hast much hidden intercourse with the soul, which is wholly hidden from her, and that Thou dost secretly attract the soul, and dost leisurely initiate her into the love and knowledge of Thy high divinity, her who at first was only concerned with Thy fair humanity.

## 10
# THE THIRD THING.

**Why God Permits His Friends To Suffer So Much Temporal Suffering**

*The Servant.*—Another thing, Lord, I have at my heart: may I venture to tell it Thee? May I indeed venture to dispute with Thee like holy Jeremias? Gentle Lord, be not angry, but listen patiently to me. Lord, people say as follows: that how sweet soever Thy love may be, Thou dost yet allow it to prove very harsh to Thy friends in the many severe trials which Thou sendest them, such as worldly scorn and much adversity, both inwardly and outwardly. Scarcely is any one, say they, admitted to Thy friendship, but he has forthwith to gather up his courage for suffering. Lord, by Thy goodness! what sweetness can they have in all this? Or how canst Thou permit it in Thy friends? Or art Thou pleased not to know anything about it?

*Eternal Wisdom.*—Even as My Father loves Me, so do I love My friends. I do to My friends now as I have done from the beginning of the world.

*The Servant.*—This is what they complain of; and therefore, say they, Thou hast so few friends because Thou allowest them to prosper in this world so very sorrily. Lord, on this account there are also indeed many who, when they gain Thy friendship, and ought to prove constant in suffering, fall off from Thee; and (woe is me! that I must say it in sorrow of heart, and with bitter tears) relapse to that state which, through Thee, they had forsaken. O my Lord, what hast Thou to say to this?

*Eternal Wisdom.*—This is the complaint of persons of a sick faith and of small works, of a lukewarm life, and undisciplined spirit. But thou, beloved soul, up with thy mind out of the slime and deep slough of carnal delights! Unlock thy interior sense, open thy spiritual eyes and see. Mark well what thou art, where thou art, and whither thou dost belong; for then shalt thou understand that I do the very best for My friends. According to thy natural essence thou art a mirror of the Divinity, thou art an image of the Trinity, and a copy of eternity; for as I, in My eternal uncreated entity, am the good which is infinite, so art thou according to thy desires, fathomless, and as little as a small drop can yield in the vast depth of the sea, just so little can all that this world is able to afford contribute to the fulfillment of thy desires. Thus, then, art thou in this wretched valley of tears, where joy and sorrow, laughing and weeping, mirth and sadness, are mingled together; where no heart ever obtained perfect happiness; for it is false and deceitful, more than I will tell thee. It promises much and performs little; it is short, uncertain, and changeable; to-day much joy, to-morrow a heart full of woe. Behold, such is the disport of this scene of time!

## 11
# ON THE EVERLASTING PAINS OF HELL

*Eternal Wisdom.*—O my chosen one! now look from the very bottom of thy heart at this lamentable misery. Where are now all those who heretofore sat down amidst this temporal scene with tranquility and pleasure, with tenderness and comfort of body? What avails them all the joys of this world which are as soon vanished on the wings of swift time as though they had never been? How quickly over is that carnal love for which pain must be eternally endured! O ye senseless fools! Where is now what ye so gaily uttered: "Hail, ye children of merriment, let us give holiday to sorrow, let us cherish the fulness of joy!" What avail now all the pleasures ye ever obtained? Well may ye cry aloud with sorrowful voice: Woe upon us that ever we were born into the world! How has swift time deceived us! How has death stolen upon us! Is there any one still upon the earth who could be more deceived than we have been deceived? Or is there any one willing to take counsel from the calamity of others? If any one were to bear all the sufferings of all mankind for a thousand years it would only be as a moment against this! How very happy is that man who has never sought after pleasures displeasing to God, who for His sake has renounced all temporal delights! We foolish ones, we deemed such men forsaken and forgotten of God: but see how He has embraced them in eternity with such marks of honour before all the heavenly host. What harm can all their sufferings and disgraces now do them, which have turned out so much to their joy? Meanwhile, all that we so entirely loved, how is it vanished! Ah, misery on misery! and it must last for ever. Oh, for ever and ever, what are thou? Oh, end without end! Oh, dying above all dying, to be dying every hour, and yet never to die. Oh, father and mother, and all that we ever held dear, God bless you for ever and ever, for we shall never see you and love you again: we must ever be separated from you. Oh, separation, oh, everlasting separation, how grievous thou art! Oh, wringing of hands, oh, fretting, sobbing, and weeping, oh, shrieking and howling for ever, and yet never to be heard!

Nothing but sorrow and distress must our wretched eyes behold, our ears be filled with nothing—but alas! nothing save only Woe is me! Oh, all hearts, let our lamentable For ever and ever! move your compassion, let our miserable For ever! pierce to your core. Oh, ye mountains and valleys, why do ye wait for us, why do ye keep us so long, why do ye bear with us, why do ye not bury us from the lamentable sight? Oh, sufferings of that world and sufferings of this world, how very different ye are! Oh, time present, how blinding, how deceiving thou art, that we should not have foreseen this in the bright days of our youth, which we wasted so luxuriously, which will never more return! Oh, that we had but one little hour of all those vanished years! Yet this is denied by God's justice, and without any hope for us, ever must be denied. Oh, suffering, and distress, and misery, in this forgotten land, where we must be separated from all that is dear, without solace or hope, for ever and ever! Nothing else would we desire than that if there was a millstone as broad as the whole earth, and in circumference so large that it everywhere touched the heavens, and that if there came a little bird every hundred thousand years, and took from the stone as much as the tenth part of a grain of millet, so as in ten hundred thousand years to peck away from the stone as much as an entire grain of millet; we unfortunates would desire nothing more than that, when the stone came to an end, our torments too might terminate; and yet even this cannot be. Behold, such is the song of woe which succeeds the joys of this world.

*The Servant.*—Oh, Thou severe Judge, how terrified are the depths of my heart, how powerless sinks my soul beneath the load of sorrow and compassion for those unhappy spirits! Who is there in the world that hears this, and is so insane as not to tremble at such fearful distress? Oh, Thou, my only love, forsake me not! Oh, Thou, my only chosen consolation, do not thus separate from me! Sooner than be thus separated from Thee, my only love, for ever and ever (I will say nothing of the rest), oh, misery of misery! I would prefer to be tormented a thousand times a day. When I but think of such a separation, my heart for anguish is like to break. Yes, tender Father! do with me here what Thou wilt, Thou hast my free consent, but, oh, deliver me from this woeful separation, for I could by no means endure it.

*Eternal Wisdom.*—Cast away thy fear. That which is united in time remains undivided in eternity.

*The Servant.*—Oh, Lord, would that all men heard this, who still consume their days so foolishly, so that they might become wise, and might reform their lives, before these things should overtake them. Oh, ye senseless, obdurate men! how long will ye protract your foolish, sinful lives? Be converted to God, and shield yourselves against this wretched misery, and lamentation of eternal woe.

## 12
## ON THE IMMEASURABLE JOYS OF HEAVEN

*Eternal Wisdom.*—Now lift up thy eyes and see where thou dost belong. Thou dost belong to the Fatherland of the celestial paradise. Thou art here as a stranger guest, a miserable pilgrim; therefore, as a pilgrim hastens back to his home where his dear friends expect him, and wait for him with great longing, so shouldst thou desire to hasten back to thy fatherland, where all will be glad to see thee, where all long so ardently for thy joyous presence, that they may greet thee tenderly, and unite thee to their blessed society for ever. And didst thou but know how they thirst after thee, how they desire that thou shouldst combat devoutly in suffering, and behave chivalrously in all adversity, even such as they have overcome, and how they now with great sweetness remember the cruel years through which they once passed, truly, all suffering would only be the easier to thee, for, the more bitterly thou shalt have suffered, the more honourably wilt thou be received. Oh, then, how pleasant will honour be, what joy will then pervade thy heart and mind when thy soul shall be so honourably praised, commended, and extolled by Me before My Father and all the heavenly host, because she has suffered so much, and fought against and overcome so much in this scene of temporal strife, in whose fulness of reward many a one who has never known affliction will have no participation. How brightly will not then the crown shine that here below is gained with such bitterness! How exquisitely beautiful will not the wounds and marks glitter, which here below are received from My love! So welcome wilt thou be made in thy fatherland, that the greatest stranger to thee of all its countless hosts will love thee more ardently and faithfully than any father or mother ever loved the child of their bosom in this scene of time.

*The Servant.*—O Lord, through Thy goodness, dare I hope that Thou wilt tell me yet more about my fatherland, so that I may long for it all the more, and may suffer every affliction the more cheerfully? Yes, my Lord, what manner of place is my fatherland? Or what do people do there? Or are there very many people there? Or do they really know so well what takes place with us on earth as Thy words declare?

*Eternal Wisdom.*—Now, then, ascend thou on high with Me. I will carry thee thither in spirit, and will give thee, after a rude similitude, a distant glimpse into the future. Behold, above the ninth heaven, which is incalculably more than a hundred thousand times larger than the entire earth, there is another heaven which is called Coelum Empyreum, the fiery heaven, so called, not from its being of fire, but from its immeasurably transparent brightness, which is immovable and unchangeable in its nature; and this is the glorious court in which the heavenly hosts dwell, where the morning star with the rest praises Me, and all the children of God rejoice. There stand, encompassed with inconceivable light, the everlasting thrones, from which the evil spirits were hurled, in which the elect are seated. See how the delightful city shines with beaten gold, how it glitters with costly jewels, inlaid with precious stones, transparent as crystal, reflecting red roses, white lilies, and all living flowers. Now, look on the beautiful heavenly fields themselves. Lo! here all delights of summer, here sunny meads of May, here the very valley of bliss, here the glad moments are seen flitting from joy to joy; here harps and viols, here singing, and leaping, and dancing, hand in hand for ever! here the gratification of every desire, here pleasure without pain in everlasting security! Now, look how the countless multitude drink to their hearts' desire at the living fountains of gushing water; look how they feast their eyes on the pure, clear mirror of the revealed Divinity, in which all things are made plain and evident to them. Steal a little nearer, and mark how the sweet queen of the celestial kingdom, whom thou lovest with so much ardour, soars aloft in dignity and joy over the whole celestial host, reclining tenderly on her beloved, encircled with rose-flowers and lilies of the valley. See how her ravishing beauty fills with delight and wonder all the heavenly choirs. Oh, now behold what will rejoice thy heart and soul, and see how the mother of compassion has turned her compassionate eyes towards thee and all sinners, and how powerfully she appeals to her beloved Son, and intercedes with Him. Now, turn round with the eyes of thy pure understanding, and behold also how the high seraphim and the love-abounding souls of the seraphic choirs blaze up perpetually in Me; how the bright company of the cherubim have a bright infusion and effusion of My eternal inconceivable light, how the high thrones and hosts, enjoy in Me a sweet repose, and I in them! Then see how the triplicity of the other hosts, the lordships, powers, and dominations, regularly fulfill My beautiful and eternal order in the universality of nature. Mark, too, how the third host of angelic spirits executes My high messages and decrees in the particular parts of the world; and see, how lovingly, how joyfully, and variously the multitude is marshalled, and what a beautiful sight it is! Turn next thy glance and see how My chosen disciples and best beloved friends sit in repose and honour upon their awful judgment-seats, how the martyrs glitter in their rose-coloured garments, the confessors shine in their vernal beauty, how refulgent the virgins appear in their angelic purity, how all the heavenly host overflows with divine sweetness! Oh, what a company! Oh, what a joyous band! Blessed, thrice blessed is he who was born to dwell where they dwell! Lo, to this very fatherland I shall carry home from misery and tribulation, arrayed in all the richness of her rich morning gift, My beloved bride in My arms. I shall adorn her interiorly with the beautiful garment of the eternal light of that glory which will exalt her above all her natural powers. She will be clothed exteriorly with the glorified body, which is seven times brighter than the sun's light, swift, subtle, and to suffering, impassive; then I shall put on her the crown of delight, and on the crown a golden garland.

*The Servant.*—Gentle Lord, what is the

morning gift, and what the crown and golden garland?

*Eternal Wisdom.*—The morning gift is a clear vision of that which here below thou dost merely believe in, an actual comprehending of that which now thou hopest for, and a heartfelt pleasant enjoyment of that which on earth thou lovest. As to the beautiful crown, it is essential reward, but the blooming garland is accidental reward.

*The Servant.*—Lord, what is that?

*Eternal Wisdom.*—ACCIDENTAL REWARD consists in such particular delight as souls obtain by particular and meritorious works wherewith they have conquered here below, even as the souls of great doctors, steadfast martyrs, and pure virgins. But ESSENTIAL reward consists in the contemplative union of the soul with the pure Divinity, for rest she never can till she be borne above all her powers and capacities, and introduced to the natural entity of the Persons, and to the clear vision of their real essence. And in the emanation of the splendour of Their essence she will find full and perfect satisfaction and everlasting happiness; and the more disengaged and abstracted the self-egression of such souls is, the more free will be their soaring exaltation; and the more free their exaltation, the deeper will be their penetration into the vast wilderness and unfathomable abyss of the unknown Godhead, wherein they are immersed, overflowed, and blended up, * so that they desire to have no other will than God's will, and that they become the very same that God is: in other words, that they be made blessed by grace as He is by nature. Raise then thy countenance joyfully, forget for a while all thy tribulations, comfort thy heart in this dark silent scene with the secret vision which thou now enjoyest of the society of the blessed, and behold how blooming and fair those faces appear which here on earth were so often red with shame for My sake; lift up thy glad heart and speak as follows: Where now is that bitter shame which so cruelly pierced your pure hearts? Where now the bowed heads, the cast down eyes? where the suppressed sorrow of heart, the deep sighs and bitter tears? where the pale looks, the dire poverty, and manifold infirmities? Where is now the miserable voice thus speaking: "Alas, my Lord and my God, how sad at heart I am!" Where are all those now who so greatly oppressed and despised you? No more are heard such words at these: "Ho, for the combat! ho, for the strife! be ready day and night like one who fights against the heathen!" Where is now what you were wont, in the presence of

---

* Without prejudice, however, to their own individuality, as Suso elsewhere clearly teaches.

grace, to say a thousand times interiorly: "Art thou prepared to combat steadily when forsaken?" No more is heard the sad and lamentable cry which you so often uttered: "O God, why hast Thou forsaken me!" Rather do I hear the sweet words lovingly sounding in your ears: "Come hither to Me, My blessed ones, possess the everlasting kingdom prepared for you from the beginning of the world." Where is now all the sorrow and affliction which ye ever endured on earth? O God, how swiftly is it all vanished like a dream as though ye had never known tribulation! Of a truth, gentle Lord, how inscrutable are Thy judgments to the world! Happy you, ye elect, it is all over now with dwelling in nooks and corners, with stealing away and hiding yourselves from the senseless follies of other men. Oh, if all hearts were but one heart, they could not sufficiently reflect on the great honour, the immeasurable deserts, the praise which you will evermore possess. O ye heavenly princes, O ye noble kings and emperors, O ye eternal children of God, how full of joy are your countenances, how full of gladness your hearts! What a loftiness of soul ye have! How right cheerfully do your voices swell forth in this song: Praise and thanksgiving, glory and benediction, grace and joy and everlasting honour to Him, from world to world, from eternity to eternity, from the very bottom of our hearts, to

Him by whose goodness we possess all these things for ever and ever! Amen! Lo, here is our fatherland, here is heartfelt jubilation, here is unfathomable everlasting life!

*The Servant.*—O wonder above all wonders! Ah, fathomless good, what art Thou? Yes, my gentle Lord, my chosen One, how good it is to be here! O my only Love, let us tarry here!

*Eternal Wisdom.*—It is not yet time to tarry here. Many a sharp conflict hast thou still to endure. This vision has only been shown to thee that thou mayest presently revert to it in all thy sufferings, as thus thou canst never lose courage, and wilt forget all thy sorrow; and further, as an answer to the complaint of foolish men who say that I allow My friends to fare so hard. See then what a difference there is between My friendship and the friendship of this temporal state; and to speak according to the truth, how much better than others My friends fare at My hands. I will say nothing of the great trouble, labour, and many a severe tribulation in which they swim and wade, night and day; only this, that they are so blinded they do not understand it. It is indeed My eternal economy that a mind not regulated should be a sharp torment and heavy burden to itself. My friends have bodily distress, but then they have peace of heart. The friends of the world hunt after bodily comfort and ease, but in their hearts, their souls and minds, they gain nothing but trouble and vexation.

*The Servant.*—Those persons, Lord, are out of their right senses, and are raving, who would needs compare Thy faithful friendship and the world's friendship together. That they should do so because Thou hast few friends who have no suffering to complain of, is the fault of their great blindness. O Lord, how very soft and gentle is Thy Fatherly rod! Blessed is he on whom Thou sparest it not. Lord, I now plainly see that tribulation does not proceed from Thy harshness, but rather from Thy tender love. Let no one say for the future that Thou hast forgotten Thy friends. Those hast Thou forgotten (for Thou hast despaired of them), on whom Thou dost spare chastisement here below. Lord, in all fairness those ought not to have joyous days, nor pleasures, nor comfort here below, whom Thou dost intend to shield above from eternal misery, and endow with everlasting delight. Grant, O Lord, that these two visions may never disappear from the eyes of my heart, so that I never may lose Thy friendship.

## 13
# ON THE IMMEASURABLE DIGNITY OF TEMPORAL SUFFERING

*The Servant.*—Tell me now, tender Lord, what this suffering is which Thou thinkest so very profitable and good?

*Eternal Wisdom.*—What I mean is every kind of suffering, whether willingly accepted or unwillingly incurred—as when a man makes a virtue of necessity in not wishing to be exempt from suffering without My will, and ordering it, in humble patience, to My eternal praise; and the more willingly he does this, the more precious and agreeable it is to Me. Touching such kinds of suffering, hear further, and write it down in the bottom of thy heart, and keep it as a sign to set before the spiritual eyes of thy soul. My dwelling is in the pure soul as in a paradise of delights, for which reason I cannot endure that she should lovingly and longingly attach herself to anything. But, from her very nature, she is inclined to pernicious lusts, and therefore I encompass her path with thorns. I garnish all her outlets with adversity, whether she like it or not, so that she may not escape from Me; her ways I strew with tribulation, so that she may not set the foot of her heart's desire anywhere except in the loftiness of My divine nature. And if all hearts were but one heart, they would not be able to bear even that least reward which I certainly will give for the suffering endured by anyone for love of Me. Such is My eternal order in all nature, from which I do not swerve; what is precious and good must be earned with bitterness; he who recoils at this, let him recoil; many are indeed called, but few are chosen.

*The Servant.*—It may well be, Lord, that suffering is an infinite good, provided it be not without measure, and not too dreadful and overwhelming. Lord, Thou alone knowest all hidden things, and didst create all things in weight, in number and measure; Thou knowest also that my sufferings are measureless, that they are wholly beyond my strength. Lord, is there anyone in all this world who has constantly more painful sufferings than I? They are to me invincible—how am I to endure them? Lord, if Thou wouldst send me ordinary sufferings, I could bear them, but I do not see how I can ever endure such extraordinary sufferings as these—sufferings which in so hidden a manner oppress my heart and soul, which only Thou canst perfectly understand.

*Eternal Wisdom.*—Every sick man imagines that his own sickness is the worst, and every man in distress, his own distress the greatest. Had I sent thee other sufferings it would have been the same. Conform thyself freely to My will under every pain which I ordain thee to suffer, without excepting this or the other suffering. Dost thou not know that I only desire what is best for thee, even with as kindly a feeling as thou thyself? Hence it is that I am the Eternal Wisdom, and that I know better than thou what is for thy good. Hence it is that thou mayst have felt that the sufferings which I send are much more exquisite, and penetrate deeper, and operate better, for him who does them justice, than all self-chosen sufferings. Why then dost thou so complain to Me? Address Me rather as follows: O my most faithful Father, do to me at all times what Thou wilt!

*The Servant.*—O Lord, it is so easy to talk, but the reality is so difficult to endure, for it is so very painful.

*Eternal Wisdom.*—If suffering gave no pain, it could not be called suffering. There is nothing more painful than suffering, and nothing more joyful than to have suffered. Suffering is a short pain and a long joy. Suffering gives to the sufferer pain here and joy hereafter. Suffering kills suffering. Suffering is ordained that the sufferer may not suffer eternally. Hadst thou so much spiritual sweetness and divine consolation and heavenly delight as, at all times, to overflow with the divine dew, it would not be for thee so very meritorious of itself, since, for all this together, I should not have to thank thee so much; it could not exculpate thee so much as an affectionate suffering or patience in adversity, in which thou sufferest for My sake. Sooner will ten be perverted and ruined in the midst of a great delight and joyous sweetness than one in the midst of constant suffering and adversity. If thou hadst as much science as all the astronomers, if thou couldst discourse as ably of God as all the tongues of men and angels, and didst possess the treasures of knowledge of all the masters, not all this could avail to advance thee in a good life, so much as if thou didst give thyself up, and didst abandon thyself in all thy sufferings to God; for the former is common to the good and the bad, but the latter is proper to My elect alone. If anyone were able rightly to weigh time and eternity, he ought rather to desire to lie in a fiery furnace for a hundred years than to be deprived in eternity of the smallest reward for the smallest suffering; for this has an end, but the other is without end.

*The Servant.*—Ah, sweet and dear Lord, how like a sweet harp are these words to a suffering mortal! Lord, Lord, wouldst Thou but cheer me thus and come to visit me in my sufferings, I should be glad to suffer; it would then be better for me to suffer than not to suffer.

*Eternal Wisdom.*—Now, then, hearken to the sweet music of the distended strings of that Divine harp—a God-suffering man—how richly it sounds, how sweetly it vibrates. Before the world, suffering is a reproach, but before Me it is an infinite honour. Suffering is an extinguisher of My wrath, and an obtainer of My favour. Suffering makes a man in My sight worthy of love, for the sufferer is like Me. Suffering is a hidden treasure which no one can make good; and though a man might kneel before Me a hundred years to beg a friendly suffering, he nevertheless would not earn it. Suffering changes an earthly man into a heavenly man. Suffering brings with it the estrangement of the world, but confers, instead, My intimate familiarity. It lessens delight and increases grace. He to whom I am to show Myself a friend, must be wholly disclaimed and abandoned by the world. Suffering is the surest way, the nearest way, and the shortest way. He who rightly knows how profitable suffering is, ought to receive it as a gift worthy of God. Oh, how many a man there is who once was a child of eternal death, and plunged in the profoundest sleep, whom suffering has wakened up and encouraged to a good life. How many a wild beast, how many an untamed bird, there is in human form, whom constant suffering has shut up, as it were, in a cage, who, if any one were to leave him time and place free, would do his best to escape from his salvation. Suffering is a safeguard against grievous falls; it makes a man know himself, rely on himself, and have faith in his neighbour. Suffering keeps the soul humble and teaches patience. It is the guardian of purity, and confers the crown of eternal salvation. There is probably no man living but who derives good from suffering, whether he be in a state of sin, or on the eve of conversion, or in the fruition of grace, or on the summit of perfection; for it purges the soul as fire purges iron and purifies gold; it adorns the wrought jewel. Suffering takes away sin, lessens the fire of purgatory, expels temptation, consumes imperfections, and renovates the spirit. It imparts true confidence, a clear conscience, and constant loftiness of mind. Know that it is a healthy beverage, and a wholesome herb above all the herbs of paradise. It chastises the body which, at any rate, must rot away, but it nourishes the noble soul which shall endure for ever. Behold, the noble soul blooms by suffering even as the beautiful rose by the fresh dews of May! Suffering makes a wise mind and an experienced man. A man who has not suffered what does he know? Suffering is affection's rod, a paternal blow given to My elect. Suffering draws and forces men to God, whether they like it or not. He who is always cheerful in suffering, has for his servants joy and sorrow, friend and foe. How often hast thou not thrust an iron bit between the gnashing teeth of thy enemies, and rendered them, with thy joyous praise, and thy meekness in suffering, powerless? Sooner would I create suffering out of nothing than leave my friends unprovided with it; for in suffering, every virtue is preserved, man adorned, his neighbour reformed, and God praised. Patience in suffering is a living sacrifice, it is a sweet smell of balsam before My divine face, it is an appealing wonder before the entire host of heaven. Never was a skillful knight in a tournament so gazed at as a man who suffers well is gazed at by all the heavenly court. All the saints are on the side of the suffering man; for, indeed, they have all partaken of it before him, and they call out to him with one voice that it contains no poison, but is a wholesome beverage. Patience in suffering is superior to raising the dead, or the performing of other miracles. It is a narrow way which leads direct to the gates of heaven. Suffering makes us companions of the martyrs, it carries honour with it, and leads to victory against every foe. Suffering clothes the soul in garments of rose colour, and in the brightness of purple; in suffering she wears the garland of red roses, and carries the sceptre of green palms. Suffering is for her as a shining ruby in a young maiden's necklace. Adorned with it, she sings with a sweet voice and a free heart a new song which not all the angelic choirs could ever sing, because they never knew suffering. And, to be short, those who suffer are called the poor before the world, but before Me they are called the blessed, for they are My elect.

*The Servant.*—Oh, how plainly does it appear that Thou art the Eternal Wisdom, since Thou canst bring the truth home with such cogency that no one doubts it any longer. No wonder that he, to whom Thou dost make suffering appear so lovely, can bear sufferings. Lord, in consequence of Thy words, all sufferings in future must be easier and full of joy for me. Lord, my true Father, behold, I kneel before Thee this day, and praise Thee fervently for my present sufferings, and also for the measureless sufferings of the past, which I deemed so very great, because they appeared so hostile to me.

*Eternal Wisdom.*—But what is thy opinion now?

*The Servant.*—Lord, my opinion in very truth is this: that when I look at Thee, Thou delight of my eyes, with looks of love, the great and violent sufferings with which, in so paternal a manner, Thou hast disciplined me, and at the sight of which Thy pious friends were filled with such terror on my account, have been like a sweet fall of dew in May.

(Now, when the same preacher had begun to write on suffering, there appeared to him, in the way already mentioned above, the same two persons that were in sorrow and trouble, sitting before him, and one of them prayed him to play on the harp to her. This he took amiss, and answered that it would be an unpriestly thing. Then he was told that it would not be unpriestly, and presently there entered a youth who prepared a harp, and when he had turned it, he spun the two threads crosswise over the strings, and gave it into the hands of the brother, and then the brother began to write on suffering).

## 14
## ON THE UNSPEAKABLE ADVANTAGES TO BE DERIVED FROM MEDITATING ON THE DIVINE PASSION

*The Servant.*—Truly, Lord, the unfathomable good which is found in Thy Passion for those who avail themselves of the time and place to meditate on it is a thing hidden from all hearts. Oh, what a sure path is the way of Thy Passion, along the way of truth, up to the very pinnacle of all perfection. All hail to thee, glorious St Paul! thou noble light among all the stars of heaven, who was wrapt up so high and initiated so deeply into the mysteries of the Godhead, when thou didst hear the deep words which it is not given to man to utter, and who yet wast so sweetly touched in thy heart by this very passion of infinite love, above everything else, that thou didst exclaim: "I determined not to know anything among you save Jesus Christ and Him crucified."* Blessed be thou, too, among all doctors, sweet St. Bernard, whose soul was so illuminated with the brightness of the eternal Word that most sweetly did thy tongue exhale from a full heart the passion of His humility, when thy fervent soul thus spoke: The green bunch of myrrh of my Lord's bitter Passion have I fondly taken betwixt my breasts, and tenderly pressed to my heart; I do not ask, like the bride, *where He rests at noon* whom I embrace in the midst of my heart: I do not ask *where He feeds His flock at noon*, whom my soul so longingly beholds on the cross; that is certainly loftier, but this is sweeter and easier to attain. From this love-o'erflowing Passion, I take what fully makes up for the insufficiency of my own small merits; herein lies my complete justification; to meditate on this Passion, I call eternal wisdom, the perfection of all knowledge, the riches of all salvation, an entire satisfaction of all desert; it casts me down in prosperity, it raises me up in adversity, it keeps me in an even balance between this world's weal and woe, and guards me against all evil in complete security. Sometimes I have drunk out of it a draught of salutary bitterness, but at other times I have also drunk out of it a draught of spiritual

---

* 1 Cor. ii.2

consolation and divine sweetness.* O sweet St. Bernard, therefore is it but just that thy tongue should overflow with sweetness, since thy heart was so wholly sweetened with sweet suffering. O Eternal Wisdom, in this, I observe that, whoever is desirous of great reward and everlasting salvation, of high knowledge and deep wisdom, of standing erect in joy and sorrow, of possessing full security against all evil, whoever wishes to drink a draught of Thy bitter Passion, and Thy singular sweetness, must carry Thee at all times, O crucified Jesus, before the eyes of his heart.

*Eternal Wisdom.*—Thou dost not rightly know what good is lodged in it. Behold, assiduous meditation on My Passion makes out of a simple man a master of high knowledge; truly it is a living book in which everything is to be found. How right blessed is that man who has it ever before his eyes and studies it! What wisdom, grace, consolation, sweetness, what cleansing from all imperfection, may not such a man obtain through the devout contemplation of My living presence! Respecting which, listen to what follows. It fell out many years ago, that a certain preacher in the beginning of his conversion had a bitter affliction of inordinate despondency, which, at times, so

---

* Sancti Bernardi Sermones in Cantica Canticorum. Sermo xliii.

overpowered him that no heart which had not experienced it could conceive it. And, as he once sat after meat in his cell, his affliction was so great that he could neither study nor pray, nor perform any other good deed, except sitting there so sadly in his cell, and laying his hands in his lap, as though he meant only to take care of the cell, for God's sake, because he was no longer of any use in spiritual things. And, as he thus sat disconsolate, it suddenly seemed to him as though he heard these words distinctly addressed to him: Why dost thou sit here? Arise and betake thee to My sorrowful Passion, for then wilt thou overcome thy own sorrow. And immediately he arose, for the words were the same to him as though they came from heaven, and he began to meditate on the sorrowful Passion of the Lord, in which all his own sorrow was lost, so that he never felt it again in the same manner.

*The Servant.*—O my sweet Wisdom, Thou understandest all hearts, and knowest that, above all things, I desire to have my heart penetrated with Thy Passion, in the face of all men, and my eyes turned day and night into running fountains of bitter tears. Alas! there is just now in my soul a bitter complaint, that Thy Passion does not at all times thoroughly penetrate my heart, and that I do not meditate on it so affectionately as in reason I ought to do, and as is worthy of Thee, my Lord elect; teach me, therefore, how I ought to comport myself!

*Eternal Wisdom.*—The meditation on My torments must not be made by going through them in a hasty manner, when one has time and opportunity, but it must be made by going through them with heartfelt love and a compassionate searching into their mysteries; for, otherwise, the heart remains as unaffected by devotion, as the mouth by unchewed sweet-tasting food. If thou hast no liking to meditate on My Passion with weeping eyes, because of the bitter agony I suffered, then oughtest thou to meditate on it with a laughing heart, because of the joyous benefit thou wilt find in it. But if thou hast no mind either to laugh or to cry, thou oughtest to meditate on it in the dryness of thy heart, to My honour and praise, by doing which thou wilt have done no less than if thou hadst been dissolved in tears or steeped in sweetness; for then thou actest from love of virtue, without regard to thyself. And that thou mayest take it all the more to heart, listen to what follows. Such is My severe justice that it permits no wrong deed in all nature, be it great or small, to pass without atonement and without being made good. Now, how should a great sinner, who has perhaps committed more than a hundred mortal sins, and for every mortal sin subjected himself, by the law of My Church, to do penance seven years long, or else to complete his unperformed penance in the furnace of grim purgatory—how should such a miserable soul fulfill her penance? When would there be an end to her sighs and tears? Oh, how long, how much too long, would it not appear to her! Behold, she has speedily made all good by means of My innocent, meritorious Passion! With reason, then, let her grasp the treasure of My acquired merits, and apply it to herself, in virtue of which, even if she ought to burn a thousand years in Purgatory, she will be able, in a short time, to discharge her guilt and penance, so as to attain heaven without any purgatory at all.

*The Servant.*—O tender and Eternal Wisdom, teach me this in Thy goodness; how glad should I be to make such a grasp!

*Eternal Wisdom.*—The way to make such a grasp is this. Let a man often and seriously weigh with a penitent heart the greatness and multitude of his evil deeds, by which he has so wantonly incensed the eyes of his Heavenly Father; in the next place, let him account as nothing the works of his own satisfaction, since, reckoned against his sins, they are but as a little drop in the deep ocean; and then, let him confidently weigh the immeasurable greatness of My satisfaction; for the least drop of My precious Blood, which everywhere flowed without measure out of My body, would alone suffice to atone for the sins of a thousand worlds. Every man, therefore, appropriates so much of My satisfaction to himself, in proportion as he assimilates himself to Me by sympathetic participation in My sufferings. Moreover let a man humbly and modestly merge the smallness of his works in the greatness of My satisfaction or atonement. And to tell it thee in a few words, know then, that all the masters of numbers and measures would be unable to calculate the immeasurable benefit which lies hidden in the zealous meditation of My Passion.

## 15
# FROM THE FOND CARESSES

**Which The Soul Has Has With God Beneath The Cross, She Returns Again To His Passion.**

*The Servant.*—Thou hast revealed to me the measureless sufferings which Thou didst suffer in Thy exterior Man on the gibbet of the cross, how cruelly tormented Thou wast, and encompassed about with the bands of miserable death. Alas! Lord, how was it beneath the cross? Or was there not one at its foot whose heart was pierced by Thy woeful death? Or how didst Thou bear Thyself in Thy sufferings towards Thy sorrowing Mother?

*Eternal Wisdom.*—Oh, listen now to a woeful thing, and let it sink into thy heart. When, as thou hast heard, I hung suspended in mortal anguish before them, behold, they stood over against Me, and, with their voices, called out scoffingly to Me, wagging their heads contemptuously, and scorning Me utterly in their hearts, as though I had been a loathsome worm. But I was firm amidst it all, and prayed fervently for them to My heavenly Father; behold, I, the innocent Lamb, was likened to the guilty thieves; by one of these was I reviled, but by the other invoked. I listened to his prayer and forgave him all his evil deeds. I opened to him the celestial paradise. Hearken to a lamentable thing. I gazed around Me and found Myself utterly abandoned by all mankind, and those very friends who had followed Me, stood now afar off; yea, My beloved disciples had all fled from Me. Thus was I left naked, and stripped of all My clothes. I had lost all power and was without victory. They treated Me without pity, but I bore Myself like a meek and silent lamb. On whichever side I turned I was encompassed by bitter distress of heart. Below Me stood My sorrowful Mother, who suffered in the bottom of her motherly heart all that I suffered in My body. My tender heart was, in consequence, deeply touched, because I alone knew the depth of her great sorrow, and beheld her distressful gestures and heard her lamentable words. I consoled her very tenderly at My mortal departure, and commended her to the filial care of My beloved disciple, and gave the disciple in charge to her maternal fidelity.

*The Servant.*—Ah, gentle Lord, who can here refrain from sighing inwardly, and weeping bitterly? Yes, Thou beautiful Wisdom, how could they, the fierce lions, the raging wolves, be so ungentle to Thee, Thou sweet Lamb, as to treat Thee thus? Tender God, oh, that Thy servant had but been there to represent all mankind! Oh, that I had stood up there for my Lord, or else had gone to bitter death with my only Love; or, had they not chosen to kill me with my only Love, that I yet might have embraced, with the arms of my heart, in sorrow and desolation, the hard stone socket of the cross, and, when it burst asunder for very pity, that my wretched heart, too, might have burst with the desire to follow my Beloved.

*Eternal Wisdom.*—It was by Me from all eternity ordained, that when My hour was come, I alone should drink the cup of My bitter Passion for all mankind. But thou, and all those who desire to imitate Me, deny yourselves, and take up, each of you, your own cross, and follow Me. For this dying to yourselves is as agreeable to Me as though you had actually gone with Me to bitter death itself.

*The Servant.*—Gentle Lord, teach me then, how I should die with Thee, and what my own cross is. For, truly, Lord, since Thou hast died for me, I ought not to live any more for myself.

*Eternal Wisdom.*—When thou dost strive to do thy best as well as thou dost understand it, and for so doing, dost earn scornful words and contemptuous gestures from thy fellow-men, and they so utterly despise thee in their hearts that they regard thee as unable, nay, as afraid, to revenge thyself, and still thou continuest not only firm and unshaken in thy conduct, but dost lovingly pray for thy revilers to thy heavenly Father, and dost sincerely excuse them before Him; lo! as often as thou diest thus to thyself for love of Me, so often is My own death freshly renewed and made to bloom again in thee. When thou dost keep thyself pure and innocent and still thy good works are so misrepresented, that with the joyful consent of thy own heart thou art reckoned as one of the wicked, and that from the bottom of thy heart thou art as ready to forgive all the injury thou hast received as though it never had happened, and, moreover, to be useful to and assist thy persecutors by word and deed, in imitation of My forgiveness of My crucifiers, then truly art thou crucified with thy Beloved. When thou dost renounce the love of all mankind, and all comfort and advantage, so far as thy absolute necessities will allow, the forsaken state in which thou dost then stand, forsaken by all earthly love, fills up the place of all those who forsook Me when My hour was come. When thou dost stand, for My sake, so disengaged from all thy friends in those things by means of which they are an impediment between Me and thee, even as though thy friends did not belong to thee, then art thou to Me a dear disciple and brother, standing at the foot of My cross, and helping Me to support My sufferings. The voluntary detachment of thy heart from temporal things, and its devotion to Me, clothe and adorn My nakedness. When, in every adversity which may befall thee from thy neighbour, thou art oppressed for the love of Me, and dost endure the furious wrath of all men from whichever side its blast come, how fiercely soever it come, and whether thou be right or wrong, as meekly as a silent lamb, so that, in virtue of thy meek heart, and sweet words, and gentle looks, thou disarmest the malice of the hearts of thy enemies; behold even this is the true image of My death accomplished in thee. Yes, wherever I find this likeness, what delight and satisfaction have I not then, and My heavenly Father also, in man. Oh, carry but My bitter death in the bottom of thy heart, and in thy prayers, and in the manifestation of thy works, and then wilt thou fulfill the sufferings and fidelity of My immaculate Mother and My beloved disciple.

*The Servant.*—Ah, loving Lord, my soul implores Thee to accomplish the perfect imaging of Thy miserable Passion on my body and in my soul, be it for my pleasure or my pain, to Thy highest praise and according to Thy blessed will. I desire, also, in particular, that Thou wouldst describe something more of the great sorrow of Thy sorrowing Mother, and wouldst relate to me how she bore herself in the hour that she stood under the cross.

## 16

# ON THE WORTHY PRAISE OF THE PURE QUEEN OF HEAVEN

*The Servant.*—Oh, the great riches of the Divine knowledge and wisdom! how very inscrutable are Thy judgments, and how unknown Thy ways. How many a strange way hast thou of bringing poor souls back to Thee! What were Thy thoughts, or how glad at heart must Thou not have been in Thy eternal immutability, when Thou didst so nobly create the pure, tender, illustrious creature above all pure creatures! Lord, then couldst Thou indeed say: I think the thoughts of peace. * Lord, Thou hast, out of the abyss of Thy essential goodness, reflected Thy glory interiorly to Thyself again, inasmuch as Thou hast led back to their origin all beings gone

---

* Jeremias xxix. 11

astray in their divine emanation. Yes, Heavenly Father, how should a sinful creature dare to approach Thee, unless Thou hadst given him Thy own elected child, Eternal Wisdom, for a guide? Yes, Eternal Wisdom, how should a sinful creature dare at all times to discover his uncleanness before such purity, unless indeed he took the mother of all compassion for his protectress? Eternal Wisdom! if Thou art my brother, Thou art also my Lord; if Thou art truly man, woe is me! so art Thou also truly God, and a very severe judge of evil deeds. For this reason, when our poor souls are in the narrow prison-house of fathomless sorrow of heart, and we can neither stir here nor there, nothing remains for us except to lift up our miserable eyes to thee, O chosen Queen of Heaven. Therefore, thou mirror reflecting the brightness of the eternal sun, thou hidden treasure of infinite compassion, this day do I and all penitent hearts salute thee! O ye exalted spirits, ye pure souls, stand forth, extol and praise, commend and exult in the ravishing paradise of all delight, the sublime Queen! for I am not worthy to do so, unless in her goodness she vouchsafe to allow me. O thou chosen bosom friend of God, thou fair golden crown of Eternal Wisdom, permit me, a poor sinner, even me in my weakness, to speak to thee a little in confidence. With a trembling heart, with a countenance of shame, with dejected eyes, my soul falls down before thee. O thou mother of all graces, methinks neither my soul nor any other sinful soul requires permission or a passport to repair to thee. Art thou not the immediate mediatrix of all sinners? The more sinful a soul is, the more reasonable it seems to her that she should have free access to thee; the deeper she is in wickedness, the more reason she has to press forwards to thee. Therefore, my soul, step joyfully forth! If thy great crimes drive thee away, her unfathomable goodness invites thee to draw near. O, therefore, thou only consolation of all sinful hearts, thou only refuge of guilty mortals, to whom so many a wet eye, so many a wounded, miserable heart is raised up, be a gracious mediatrix and channel of reconciliation between me and the Eternal Wisdom. O think, think, thou mild Queen elect, that thou derivest all thy merits from us poor sinners. What was it made thee God's mother, made thee a casket in which the Eternal Wisdom reposed? O Lady, it was the sins of us poor mortals! How couldst thou be called a mother of graces and compassion, except through our wretchedness, which has need of grace and compassion. Our poverty has made thee rich, our crimes have ennobled thee above all pure creatures. O turn hither then the eyes of thy compassion, which thy gentle heart never turned from a sinner, from a forlorn mortal! Take me under thy protection, for my consolation and confidence are in thee. How many a guilty soul, after having bid farewell to God and all the heavenly host, by denying God and despairing of Him, and being lamentably separated from Him, has, by still clinging to thee, been sweetly detained, till at length, through thy intercession, it has again attained to grace. Who is the sinner, how great soever his crimes, to whom thy overflowing goodness has denied assistance? Lo, when my soul seriously reflects within herself, methinks it were only right, if it were possible, that while my eyes wept for joy, my heart should leap out of my mouth; so does thy name dissolve in my mouth like honey from the comb. Even thou art called the mother, the Queen of Compassion, yes, tender mother, yes, gentle mother of compassion! O what a name! O how unfathomable is the being whose name is so rich in grace! Did ever the melody of song resound as soothingly in an agitated heart as thy pure name in our penitent hearts? At this exalted name all heads in reason ought to incline, all knees to bend. How often hast thou not put to flight the hostile powers of wicked spirits, how often hast thou not allayed the angry justice of the severe judge! How often hast thou not obtained from Him grace and consolation! Yes, poor sinful mortals as we are, what have we to say to it? How shall we ever acknowledge such great goodness? If all angelic tongues, all pure spirits and souls, if heaven and earth and all that is contained in them cannot properly praise her merits, her ravishing beauty, her graciousness and immeasurable dignity, alas! what shall we sinful hearts be able to do? Let us do our best, and express to her our acknowledgements, our thanks; for indeed her great kindness does not look at the smallness of the gift, it looks at the purity of intention. Ah, sweet Queen, with what justice may not thy sex rejoice in thy sweet name; for cursed was the first Eve that she ever eat of the bitter fruit of the tree of knowledge; blessed be the second Eve that she brought us again the sweet fruit of heaven! Let no one lament over Paradise; one paradise we lost, and have won two others. For is she not a paradise in whom grew the fruit of the living tree? in whom all delight and joy are contained together? And is not that also a paradise above every paradise in whom the dead again live, if they only taste His fruit from whose hands, feet, and side the living fountains which irrigate all the earth flow,\* the fountains of inexhaustible mercy, fathomless wisdom, overflowing sweetness, ardent love, the fountains of eternal life? Truly, Lord, whoever tastes of this

---

\* Gen. ii. 10

fruit, whoever has drunk of this fountain, knows that these two gardens of paradise far surpass the earthly paradise. But thou, O Queen elect, art the gate of all grace, the door of compassion, that never yet was shut. Heaven and earth may pass away, ere thou wilt permit anyone who earnestly seeks thy assistance to depart from thee without obtaining it. Behold, for this very reason art thou the first object my soul sees when I awake, the last when I lie down to sleep. How should anything which thy pure hands present before God and commend unto Him, how small soever in itself, be rejected? Take, O take, therefore, the smallness of my works and present it, so that, in thy hands it may appear something before the eyes of God Almighty. Even thou art the pure vessel of red gold, melted down with graces, inlaid with precious emeralds, and sapphires, and all virtues, whose single aspect, in the sight of the heavenly King, surpasses that of all other creatures. O, thou lovely divine spouse elect, if King Ahasuerus was captivated by the beauty of Esther, if she was found pleasing in his eyes above all women, if she found favour above them all, so that he did for her whatever she desired, O thou, all red roses and lilies, surpassing beauty, how justly may the King of Heaven be captivated by thy spotless purity, thy meek humility, by the sweet smelling nosegay of all thy virtues and graces! Or, who has ever caught the wild and noble unicorn, if not thou?\* How infinitely pleasing, above all mortals, in His eyes is thy delicate and love-inspiring beauty, before which all other beauty fades like a glow-worm before the brightness of the sun. What overflowing grace hast thou not found before Him for thyself and us mortals who are without grace! How should, how can, then, the Heavenly King deny thee anything? Truly mayest thou say, My Beloved is mine, and I am His. Ah! thou art God's, and God is thine, and ye two have an eternal and unfathomable reciprocation of love which no duality can divide. Think of us poor needy ones, who continue to wander so wretchedly in sorrowful affliction. Yes, exalted Lady of heaven and earth, arise now and be to us a mediatrix, and an obtainer of grace with thy tender Child, the Eternal Wisdom. Ah, Eternal Wisdom, wilt Thou deny me anything? Even as I present Thee before Thy heavenly Father, so do I present Thy pure tender mother before Thee. Look at her mild eyes which so often

---

\* According to a legend of the Middle Ages, the unicorn loves chastity so much that it can only be caught by a virgin, who in consequence lies in wait at a place where the unicorn is accustomed to seek its food, and which is no is no sooner conscious of the virgin's presence than it approaches her softly, and lays its head in her lap and falls asleep. Then she makes a sign, and the concealed hunters rush upon their prey.

looked kindly on Thee; behold Those fair cheeks which she so often affectionately pressed to Thy infant face. O look at her sweet mouth which used to kiss Thee so fondly and tenderly again and again. Look at her pure hands which so often ministered to Thee. O Thou goodness above all goodness, how canst thou deny anything to her who suckled Thee so affectionately and bore Thee in her arms; who laid Thee to rest, wakened Thee and tenderly reared Thee! O Lord, let me remind Thee of all the love Thou ever didst experience from her in Thy childhood's days, when Thou didst sit in her motherly lap, and with Thy playful eyes didst laugh so pleasantly and tenderly in her face with that fathomless love Thou hadst for her above all other creatures! Think, too, of the heart-rending woe which her maternal heart endured with Thee under the gibbet of Thy miserable cross, where she saw Thee in the agony of death, and when her heart and soul so often died away in sorrow and distress with Thee. Lord, I entreat Thee, for her sake, to grant me every means of shaking off my sins, of acquiring Thy grace, and never losing it again.

## 17

## ON THE UNUTTERABLE HEART-RENDING GRIEF OF THE PURE QUEEN OF HEAVEN

*The Servant.*—Who will give my eyes as many tears as there are letters, so that with bright tears I may write down the miserable tears of the unfathomable heart-rending grief of my Blessed Lady? Pure Lady and noble Queen of Heaven and Earth, touch my stony heart with one of thy scalding tears, one of those which thou didst shed in bitter distress for thy tender Child under the wretched cross, so that my heart of stone may be softened, and may hearken to thee; for heart-rending grief is of such a nature, that no one can have a true knowledge of it, except him whom it touches. Touch then my heart, O Lady Elect, with thy sorrowful words, and tell me in short significant terms, simply as an admonition, how it was with thee in thy mind, and how thou didst support thyself at the foot of the cross, when thou didst behold thy tender Child, the beautiful and tender Wisdom, so lamentably expire.

*Answer.*—Thou shouldst hearken to it with sorrow and heartfelt woe; for although I am now exempt from suffering, yet, at that time I was not. Before I had reached the foot of the cross, I had endured many a great unspeakable anguish of heart, especially at the spot where I first caught sight of the beating, kicking, and ill-usage of my Child, on beholding which my strength forsook me, and thus helpless was I carried after my dear Son to the foot of the cross. But, in respect of what thou askest, how I felt in my mind, and how I supported myself, listen to as much as it is possible for thee to know; for the whole no heart that ever was made can fathom. Understand, then, that all the sorrow that ever could afflict a heart would only be as a drop in the ocean compared to the unfathomable sorrow which my maternal heart at that time endured; and, understand, at the same time, that the dearer, the sweeter, the more precious the beloved one is, the more insupportable is his loss and death. Now, where on the whole earth was there ever a more tender one born, a lovelier one seen than my own best beloved one, Jesus Christ, by whom and in whom I had entire possession of all that the world could bestow? I was already dead to myself, and lived only in Him, and when at last my own fair love was slain, then only did I utterly die; and, as my only love was but one, and, moreover, dear to me above all other loves, so my only sorrow was but one, and a sorrow above all sorrows that ever were expressed. His fair and gentle humanity was, to me, a delightful spectacle; His dignified divinity was, to my eyes, a sweet contemplation; to think of Him was my heart's delight; to speak of Him was my pastime; to hear His sweet words was music to my soul. He was my heart's mirror, my soul's comfort; heaven and earth, and all that is in them, I possessed in His sweet presence. Lo, when I saw my love suspended in mortal agony before me, alas, the sight! Alas, what a moment was that! How died my heart within me! How was my courage extinguished! How did my strength fail me! How did all my senses forsake me! I looked up, but I could not help my child. I looked down, and saw only those who so cruelly ill-used Him. O how narrow then to me was all this world! I had lost all heart; my voice had fled from me; I had, moreover, lost all strength; and yet, when I came to myself, I raised thy feeble voice, and spoke to my Child, complainingly, such words as these: Alas, my Child! Alas, thou Child of mine! Alas, my heart's delightful mirror, in which I have so often taken delight to behold myself, how do I now see Thee miserably suspended before me! Alas, thou treasure above all this world! My mother, my father, and all that my heart can express (such art Thou to me), take me with Thee! Or, to whom wilt Thou leave Thy wretched mother? Oh, who will permit me to die for Thee, to suffer for Thee this bitter death? Oh, misery and distress of a love-torn mother, how am I robbed of all joy, of all love, of all consolation! Oh, thou greedy death, why sparest thou me? Take, take away the poor mother with her poor Child; to her, to live is bitterer than to die! Him, even Him, whom my soul loveth, I see dying! And as I thus lifted up my voice in lamentation, behold, my Child consoled me very affectionately, and, among other things, said: That in no other way might mankind be redeemed, and that on the third day He intended to rise again and appear to me and His disciples; and He said further: Woman, cease thy weeping; weep no more, my fair mother, I will not forsake thee for ever! And while my Child thus tenderly consoled me, and commended me to the disciple whom He loved, and who also stood by, full of sorrow (those words of His were conveyed to my heart in a tone so lamentable, and so broken by sighs, that they pierced through my heart and soul like a sharp sword), even the hard hearts of the Jews were moved to compassion for me. I cast up my arms and my hands, and, in the anguish of my heart, would gladly have embraced my beloved, yet this I might not do. And then I sank down, overwhelmed by my heart-rending grief, at the foot of the cross and became speechless; and when I returned to myself, and could do nothing else, I kissed the blood that trickled down from His wounds, so that my pale cheeks and mouth were all tinged with blood.

*The Servant.*—Ah, Thou unfathomable goodness, what infinite torture, what infinite misery is this! Whither shall I turn, or to whom shall I cast my eyes? If I look up at the beautiful Wisdom, I only see woe and distress, at which my heart is like to sink within me. They cry out and shout against Him outwardly, the agony of death struggles with Him inwardly, all His veins are on the rack, all His blood gushes away, it is nothing but ejaculations of woe, and cheerless dying without recovery. Then, if I but turn my eyes to His pure Mother, I see her tender heart pierced, alas! with wounds as though a thousand blades had transfixed it. I see her pure soul lacerated by woe. Never were such gestures of misery and longing seen as hers, never motherly lamentation heard like hers; deprived was her sick body of all strength, her fair countenance besmeared with mortified blood. Oh, great misery above all misery! The torture of His heart consists in the affliction of His sorrowing Mother; the torture of His sorrowing Mother consists in the innocent death of her beloved Son, more painful to her than her own death. He beholds her and consoles her tenderly; she stretches out her hands to Him, and would gladly die instead of Him. Alas! which of the two feels here the most bitterly? Whose is the greater distress? To both it is so unfathomable that there never was any equal to it. Alas! the motherly heart. Alas! the tender womanly mind. How was thy maternal heart ever able to support this infinite sorrow? Blessed be that heart compared to whose sorrow everything that ever was uttered of a heart's sorrow is only as a dream to the reality. Blessed be Thou, O rising blush of morning, above all creatures! And blessed be the flower-enamelled rose-scented meadow of Thy fair countenance, adorned with the ruby red blood of Eternal Wisdom! Alas! Thou affable countenance of beautiful wisdom, how dost Thou fade in death! Alas! Thou beautiful body, how dost Thou hang suspended! Woe is me, Thou pure blood, how hotly dost Thou run down on Thy pure Mother who bore Thee! Lament, ye mothers, lament with me over this affliction! All ye pure hearts, let this rose-coloured, pure blood which so besprinkles your pure Mother, go to your hearts! Behold, all hearts, ye who ever had sorrow, behold and see, if ever there was sorrow like unto this sorrow! Truly, it is a wonder that our hearts melt not here for pity and compassion; so great, indeed, was this distress, that hard stones were rent asunder, the earth trembled, the sun was extinguished, because they would fain show compassion for their Creator!

## 18
## HOW IT WAS WITH HIM AT THAT HOUR IN REGARD OF HIS INTERIOR MAN

*The Servant.*—Eternal Wisdom! the more one reflects on Thy measureless Passion, the more unfathomable it appears. Thy extremity was so very great under the cross, but still more so on the cross, according to Thy exterior powers which, at that hour, felt all the pangs of bitter death. But, gentle Lord, how was it with Thy interior Man, with Thy noble Soul? Had it no consolation, no sweetness like other martyrs' souls, so as to mitigate its cruel sufferings? Or, when did Thy sufferings come to an end?

*Eternal Wisdom.*—Now, hearken to a misery of miseries, such as thou never yet didst hear of. Although My soul, according to her highest powers, was at that time wrapt in the vision and enjoyment of the pure divinity, noble as, in truth, she is, behold, the lower powers of My exterior and interior nature were yet wholly abandoned to themselves, even to the very last drop of infinite bitterness of suffering, without any consolation, so that no torment was ever equal to it. And as I was thus left entirely helpless and forsaken, with running wounds, with weeping eyes, with extended arms, with the veins of My body on the rack, in the agony of death, then it was that I lifted up My voice in lamentation, and cried out miserably to My Father: My God, My God, why hast Thou forsaken Me? And still in all this, My will was united in eternal conformity with His will. And when all My blood was poured out, and all My strength exhausted, behold, I was seized by a bitter thirst, because of My mortal agony. But I thirsted still more for the salvation of man. Then did they reach Me vinegar and gall to quench the burning thirst of My parched mouth. And when I had accomplished the work of human redemption, I cried out: It is finished! I was entirely obedient to My Father, even unto death. My spirit I commended into His hands, saying: Into Thy hands I commend My Spirit. And then My noble Soul separated from My body, both of which yet remained unseparated from the divinity! After this a sharp spear was thrust into My right side; forthwith a stream of precious blood gushed out, and with it a fountain of living water. Behold, My child, in an extremity so pitiable as this did I redeem thee, and all the elect, and did save thee by the living sacrifice of My innocent blood from everlasting death.

*The Servant.*—Alas! tender and loving Lord and Brother, with what sorrowful, what bitter toil didst Thou not reap me in! Alas! noble Lord, how ardently didst Thou love me, how generously didst Thou redeem me! Woe is me, Thou fair Wisdom, how shall I ever be in a condition to acknowledge Thy love and Thy sufferings? If I had Samson's strength, Absalom's beauty, Solomon's wisdom, and the riches and greatness of all kings, my only wish would be to devote them to Thy praise and service. But, Lord, I am nothing, and therefore can do nothing. O Lord, how am I to thank Thee?

*Eternal Wisdom.*—If thou hadst the tongues of all the angels, the good works of all mankind, and the powers of all created beings, thou yet couldst not thank Me, nor requite Me, for the least pang which I suffered for the love of thee.

*The Servant.*—Tender Lord, inform and teach me, then, how I may become pleasing to Thee by means of Thy grace, since no one is able to make Thee a return for the tokens of Thy love.

*Eternal Wisdom.*—Thou shouldst often set My sorrowful cross before thy eyes, and let My bitter torments penetrate to thy heart, and shape thy own sufferings after them. If I allow thee to pine and wither in disconsolate affliction and dryness, without any sweetness, thou shouldst not seek after strange consolation. Let thy cry of misery rise to thy heavenly Father with a renunciation of thyself and all thy desires, according to His Fatherly will. The bitterer thy suffering is from without, and the more resigned thou art from within, the more like art thou to Me, and the more dear to My heavenly Father, for herein the most pious are put to the strongest proof. What though thy desires may have a thirsty craving to seek satisfaction and delight in something that might be pleasant to them, yet shouldst thou forego it for My sake, and thus will thy thirsty mouth be steeped with me in bitterness. Thou shouldst thirst after the salvation of men. Thy good works thou shouldst direct to a perfect life, and persevere to the end. Thy will must be subject, thy obedience prompt to thy superiors; thy soul, and all that belongs to it, thou must surrender into thy heavenly Father's hands, and thy spirit must ever be dying out of time into eternity, in prefiguration of thy last journey. Behold, thus will thy cross be shaped after My miserable cross, and worthily accomplished in it. Thou shouldst wholly lock thyself up with My love-wounded heart in My open side, and dwell there, and seek there thy resting-place. Then will I wash thee with the waters of life, and deck thee out with My precious blood, in purple. I will associate Myself to thee, and unite thee with Myself eternally.

*The Servant.*—Lord, never was there any magnet so powerful in attracting hard iron to itself, as Thy love-fraught Passion, thus presented to my soul, is powerful to unite to itself all hearts. Alas! Thou loving Lord, draw me now by means of love and sorrow away from this world to Thee on Thy cross, fulfill in me the closest resemblance to Thy cross, so that my soul may enjoy Thee in Thy highest glory.

19

## ON THE TAKING DOWN FROM THE CROSS

*The Servant.*—Ah, pure Mother and tender Lady! When did thy great and bitter affliction of heart which thou hadst for thy Son, come to an end?

*Answer.*—Listen to my words with sorrowful compassion. When my tender Child had expired, and when He hung suspended before me, and all the strength of my heart was utterly broken, though I could do nothing else, I yet cast many a glance up at my dead Child. And when they came to take Him down, it was as if I had been roused from the dead. With what motherly love did I receive His lifeless arms, with what sighs of love did I not press them to my blood-stained cheeks, and when He was lowered down to me, how affectionately beyond measure did I not embrace Him, dead as He was in my arms; how did I not strain to my heart my only love elect, and kiss again and again the fresh bleeding wounds of His face! And, yet, with what ravishing beauty His entire body was transformed, all hearts could not sufficiently contemplate. Then did I take my tender Child on to my lap, and look at Him. I looked at Him, and He was dead! I looked at Him again and again, but He had neither voice nor consciousness. Then did my heart die within me again, and had well-nigh burst into a thousand pieces. Then did I fetch many a deep and heart-rending sigh, my eyes shed many tears, my whole figure was deplorable to see, scarcely had my doleful words reached my lips, when they were choked by grief, and only half expressed. Alas, alas, cried I, whenever was anyone so cruelly used on earth as Thou, my innocent and beloved Child! Alas, my Child, my only consolation, my only joy, how art Thou changed for me into a source of much bitterness! Where is now the joy I experienced at Thy birth? Where the delight I had in Thy childhood? Where the honour and dignity I had in Thy presence? Whither is all gone that could ravish my heart? Oh sorrow! Oh anguish! Oh bitterness! Oh desolation of heart! truly is everything transformed into an unfathomable desolation of heart, into a mortal agony! Alas, Thou Child of mine, how am I so shorn of all love, how has my heart become utterly disconsolate! Such, and many such words of lamentation did I utter, because of my deceased Child.

*The Servant.*—Oh, pure and beautiful Mother, permit me once more to console my heart in this moment with thy dear Child, my Lord, the Eternal Wisdom, before the hour of separation comes, before He is snatched away from us to the grave. Immaculate Mother! however unfathomable thy heart's affliction was, however strongly it may touch all other hearts, thou didst yet, methinks, find some pleasure in the affectionate embracing of thy deceased Child. Oh, pure and gentle Lady, I desire that thou wouldst offer me thy dear Child, as He appeared in death, on the lap of my soul, so that I may experience, according to my ability, in spirit and meditation, what thou didst in thy body. Lord, my eyes are turned to Thee in the most rapturous joy and in deepest, heart-felt love, such as no only love was ever regarded with by the beloved. Lord, my soul expands to Thy embrace even as the tender rose expands to the pure sun's brightness. Lord, my soul stretches out her arms to Thee with infinite desire. Oh, my loving Lord, with ardent desire I embrace Thee to-day, and press Thee to the bottom of my heart and soul, and put Thee in mind of the loving hour of Thy death, that Thou mayest never allow it to be lost in me; and I request that neither life, nor death, nor joy, nor sorrow, may ever separate Thee from me. Lord, my eyes contemplate Thy dead countenance, my soul kisses again and again all Thy fresh bleeding wounds, all my senses are fed with this sweet fruit beneath the living tree of the cross; and it is reasonable, for this person consoles himself with his innocent life, the other with his great exercises and strict conduct; the one with this, the other with that; but, as for me, all my consolation, all my trust, are lodged wholly in Thy Passion, in Thy satisfaction and merited reward, and, therefore, I shall at all times carry Thy Passion joyfully in the bottom of my heart, and show the image of it outwardly, in words and deeds, to the utmost of my ability.

Oh, enchanting brightness of eternal light, how art Thou now for me utterly extinguished! Extinguish in me the burning lust of all vice.

Oh, pure transparent mirror of divine majesty, how art Thou now defiled! Cleanse away the great stains of my evil deeds!

Oh, beautiful image of paternal goodness, how art Thou befouled and utterly defaced! Restore the defaced and faded image of my soul!

Oh, Thou innocent Lamb, how wretchedly art Thou used! Amend and atone for my guilty, sinful life!

Oh, Thou King of all kings, and Lord of all

lords, how does my soul see Thee lying here in so lamentable and ghastly a plight! Grant, that since my soul now embraces Thee with sorrow and lamentation in Thy dereliction, she may be embraced by Thee with joy in Thy everlasting glory. Amen.

## 20
# ON THE LAMENTABLE SEPARATION OF THE GRAVE

*The Servant.*—Now, tender Lady, put an end to thy sorrow and thy sad recital, and tell me how thou didst separate from thy Beloved.

*Answer.*—It was a misery to see and hear. Alas, all was yet supportable, while I had my Child with me; but when they tore my dead Child from my blighted heart, from my embracing arms, from my face pressed to His, and buried Him, what a wailing I set up in that hour would hardly be believed; and then when it came to the separation, oh, what an agony, what woe, were seen in me! For when they separated me from my Beloved, the separating wrestled with my heart like bitter death. Supported by their hands who led me away, I walked with tottering steps, for I was robbed of all consolation, my heart longed woefully to return to my Love, my confidence was wholly set in Him, I rendered Him alone of all mankind entire fidelity and true attachment, even to the grave.

*The Servant.*—Oh, affectionate and tender Lady, for this do all hearts greet thee, all tongues praise thee, since all the good that the Fatherly heart has vouchsafed to give us, flowed through thy hands. Thou are the beginning, thou art the means, thou shalt also be the end. Alas, pure and tender Mother, let me remind thee to-day of thy miserable separation; think of thy bitter separating from thy tender Child, and help me that I may not be separated either from thee or from His joyous countenance.

Yes, pure Mother, even as my soul now stands by thee with compassionate sympathy, and embraces thee with ardent desire, and, in contemplation with heartfelt desire, with thanksgiving and praise, leads thee from the sepuchre through the gate of Jerusalem back again to thy house, so do I crave that, at my last departure, my soul may be again led by thee, O pure and tender Mother, to its Fatherland, and there be confirmed in everlasting bliss. Amen.

#  THE SECOND PART

# 1
# HOW WE SHOULD LEARN TO DIE, AND OF THE NATURE OF AN UNPROVIDED DEATH

*The Servant.*—Eternal Wisdom! if any one were to give me the whole earth for my own, it would not be so agreeable to me as the truth and the advantage which I have found in Thy sweet doctrines. Therefore, do I desire from the very bottom of my heart that Thou, the Eternal Wisdom, wouldst teach me still more. Lord, what is that which belongs, above all things, to a servant of Eternal Wisdom, who is desirous to live for Thee alone? Lord, I should like to hear about the union of pure reason with the Holy Trinity, when, in the true reflection of the eternal birth of the Word, and in the regeneration of her own Spirit, reason is ravished from herself and stands face to face with God.

*Eternal Wisdom.*—Let not him ask about what

is highest in doctrine, who still stands on what is lowest in a good life. I will teach thee what will profit thee more.

*The Servant.*—Lord, what wilt Thou teach me?

*Eternal Wisdom.*—I will teach thee to die and will teach thee to live. I will teach thee to receive Me lovingly, and will teach thee to praise Me lovingly. Behold, this is what properly belongs to thee.

*The Servant.*—Eternal Wisdom, if I had the power to fulfill my wishes, I know not whether, in this temporal state, I ought to wish anything else, as to doctrine, than how to die to myself and all the world, how to live wholly for Thee, to cherish Thy love with all my heart, to receive Thee lovingly, and to praise Thee lovingly. O God, how blessed is that man who is able to do this, and who consumes in it his whole life. But, Lord, dost Thou mean a spiritual dying or a bodily dying?

*Eternal Wisdom.*—I mean both one and the other.

*The Servant.*—What need have I, Lord, of being taught to die bodily? Surely it teaches itself when it comes.

*Eternal Wisdom.*—He who puts his teaching off till then, will find it too late.

*The Servant.*—O Lord, it is still somewhat bitter for me to hear about death.

*Eternal Wisdom.*—Behold, even this is the source of those unprovided and terrible deaths whereof the towns and convents now are full. Behold, death has often bridled thee secretly, and had fain ridden thee from hence, in the same way as he does the countless multitude, one of whom I will now show thee. Open, therefore, thy interior sense, and see and listen; see what grim death is like in the person of thy neighbour, do but mark the lamentable voice thou wilt hear.

*The Servant* heard with his understanding the voice of an unprepared dying man cry aloud and speak as follows: *The sorrows of death have surrounded me.*\* Woe is me, Thou God of Heaven, that ever I was born into the world. The beginning of my life was with crying and weeping, and now my departure from it is also with bitter crying and weeping. Alas, the sorrows of death have surrounded me, the pains of hell have encompassed me! O death, O furious death, what an unwelcome guest thou art to my young and joyous heart! How little was I prepared for thy coming! Thou hast attacked me from behind, thou hast run me down. Thou leadest me away in thy chains like one that leads a condemned man bound and fettered to the place where he is to be slain. I clasp my hands above my head, I wring

---

\* Psalm xvii. 5

them with anguish in each other, for gladly would I escape from him. I look around me into all the ends of the earth to see if any one will give me advice or help, and it cannot be. Death I hear thus fatally speaking within me: Neither learning, nor money, nor friends can avail thee; thou art mine by right. Alas, and must it be so? O God, and must I then depart from hence? Is a last separation really at hand? Woe is me that ever I was born! O death, what art thou going to do with me?

*The Servant.*—Dear man, why dost thou take it so hard? This is the common lot of rich and poor, young and old. Many more have died in their youth than in their old age. Or wouldst thou, perhaps, alone escape death? This would prove a great want of understanding in thee.

*The unprepared dying man.*—O Lord, what bitter consolation is this! I am not without understanding. Those are without understanding who have not lived for Him, and who are not frightened at death. Such persons are blind; they die like cattle; they know not what they have before them. I do not complain that I must die; I complain that I must die unprepared. I do not merely lament the end of my life, I lament and weep over the delightful days which are so utterly lost and vanished without any profit. For truly I am like an untimely and rejected abortion, like a blossom torn off in May. My days have sped swifter than an arrow from the bow. I am forgotten as though I had never been, like a track which a bird makes through the air, which closes behind it and is unknown to all men. Therefore are my words so full of bitterness, therefore is my speech so full of woe! Oh, who will enable me to be as I once was, to have again those pleasant times before me, and to know then what I know now! When those times were mine I did not rightly estimate them; I, foolish man, let them pass swiftly away; now are they vanished from me; I cannot recall them, I cannot overtake them. No hour so short but I ought to have valued it more preciously and thankfully than a poor man about to receive a kingdom as a gift. Lo, this is why my eyes shed salt tears, because they cannot restore what I have lost. Woe is me, O God; that I should have feasted so many days away, and that it profits me now so little. Why did not I learn to die all the time? O ye blooming roses, that have still your days before you, look at me and learn wisdom; turn your youth to God, and with Him alone occupy your time, so that what has happened to me may not happen to you. Ah, me! how have I consumed my youth! No one would I believe; my wayward spirit would listen to no one. Alas, now am I fallen into the snare of bitter death! My days have vanished, my youth has sped. Better were it for me had my mother's womb become my grave than that I should so have squandered away my time.

*The Servant.*—Be converted to God; repent of thy sins; if thy end be well, then will all be well.

*Unprepared dying man.*—Alas, what do I hear? How shall I do penance? How shall I now be converted to God? Seest thou not how terrified I am, how exceeding great is my distress? Even as a little bird caught in the claws of a cruel falcon, and become senseless in the agony of dying, I am unconscious of everything except that I would gladly escape and cannot. Death and the bitterness of separation oppress me. Alas, the repentance and free conversion of him who is capable of right doing, what a sure thing you are! He who puts you off will hardly fail of being himself put off. O long protraction of my amendment, how much too protracted hast thou not proved! My good intentions without works, my good promises without performance, have ruined me. I have said to God, Tomorrow and to-morrow, till I am fallen into the night of death. O Thou Almighty God, is it not a misery above all miseries, ought it not deeply to afflict me, that I should thus have lost the whole of my life, my thirty, my forty years? I know not that I ever spent a day wholly according to God's will, or that I ever rendered to God, as in reason I ought to have done, a truly acceptable service. Oh, how the thought cuts me to the heart! O God, how wretchedly shall I not stand before Thee and the whole heavenly host! Lo, now I am departing hence; and now, even at this hour, a single Pater Noster, uttered with devotion, would rejoice me more than if anyone were to put into my hands a thousand pounds of gold. Ah, my God, what have I not eternally neglected, what evil have I not inflicted on myself in not having seen this while it was in my power! What hours upon hours have escaped me! How have I allowed myself to be led wrong by small things in the great affair of my salvation! It would now be more agreeable to me, and would procure me more eternal reward if, from divine love, I had foregone the pleasure I took at the sight of a friend, when such pleasure was contrary to God's will, than if that friend were to demand a reward for me from God thirty years long on his knees. Hear, hear, all men, a lamentable thing: I go begging round and round, because my time is short, and beg a small alms out of the merits of good people as an expiation for myself, and it is refused me; for they are all afraid lest they should want oil in their lamps. Alas, Thou God of Heaven, let this move Thy compassion, that with my healthy body I could have earned such great reward and wealth on so many a day when I went about idle, and that now this small alms, begged only as an expiation, not as a reward, for which, moreover, I should stand indebted, no one will give me. Oh, let this, ye old and young, go to your hearts, and hoard up in the good season while ye can, so that ye may not become beggars, and be denied in an hour like this.

*The Servant.*—Alas, my dear friend, thy distress rends my very heart. By the living God, I conjure thee, give me some advice so that I may not come into trouble.

*The unprepared dying man.*—The best advice I can give thee, the greatest wisdom and prudence on earth, is this: That thou prepare thyself by a full confession of and an abstinence from all those things with which thou knowest thyself to be infected, and that thou hold thyself at all times ready, as though thou shouldst have to depart hence in a day, or at latest in a week. Imagine now, in thy heart, that thy soul is in Purgatory, and doomed to remain there ten years for her evil deeds, and that this year alone is granted thee to help her in. Look at her very often, see how woefully she calls out to thee and speaks to thee: O thou my best beloved friend, reach me thy hand, have pity on me, and help me to pray that I may speedily come out of this raging fire of Purgatory, for I am so miserable, that there is nobody, except thee alone, to help me, with charitable works. I am forgotten by all the world, because every one is busy about himself.

*The Servant.*—This were a choice doctrine for whoever might actually feel it like Thee in their hearts. But though Thy words are so piercing, yet do people sit here and give little heed to them; they have ears and hear not; they have eyes and see not; no one will really die before his soul departs out of him.

*The unprepared dying man.*—Wherefore, when at last they are caught on the hook of death, and cry aloud in woeful distress and cruel pain, they are not heard. Lo, even as among a hundred persons who wear the appearance of holiness (of others I will say nothing), not one pays attention to my words, that he may be converted and reform his life, so is it come to that pass that among a hundred, not one but falls into the snare of death unprepared; as also certainly happens to those who die suddenly, or in an unconscious state; for the comforts of the body, perishable love, and the greedy pursuits of sustenance, blind the multitude. But if thou wouldst be delivered from this miserable and unprovided death, then follow my advice. Behold, diligent meditation on death, and faithful assistance given to thy poor soul, who appeals so piteously to Thee, will advance thee so far that thou wilt not only be without fear, but more, thou wilt expect death with all the ardour of thy heart. Think of me every day, and write down my words in the bottom of thy heart. In my bitter distress see what thy future lot will be; look what a night this is. Oh, happy the man, that ever he was born, who arrives well prepared at this hour, for his passage will be a good one, however bitter his death; behold the bright angels will guard him, the saints escort him, the celestial court receive him; his final marching forth will be a glorious entry into his everlasting fatherland. But me, alas! where will my soul lodge this very night in that strange, mysterious country? Oh, my soul, how art thou utterly forsaken! O God, how very miserable she will be among all miserable souls! Who is there that will help her with entire fidelity? And now let me put an end to my sad complaints; for my hour is come. I see now that it cannot be otherwise. My hands begin to grow cold, my face to turn livid, my eyes to lose their sight. Alas, the shocks of furious death wrestle with my poor heart. I begin to fetch my breath very hard. The light of this world begins to vanish from me. I begin to see into the next world. O God, my God, what a sight! The horrible forms of black Moors assemble together; the wild beasts of hell surround me. They gloat over my poor soul to see if it will be theirs. O Thou just judge of the severe judgment seat, how very heavy in Thy scales are those things which in ours are so light! The cold sweat of death bursts, from very anxiety, through my flesh. Oh, the wrathful aspect of the severe judge, how very sharp Thy judgments are! Now let me turn in spirit to that world where I am led by the hand into Purgatory, and where, in the land of torments, I see anguish and distress. O God, I see the wild, hot flames dart up on high, and meet over the heads of suffering souls. They wander up and down amid the dark flames, and great is their affliction. What heart would like to contemplate our pangs, the bitterness of our woe? Many a sad cry is heard. Help! help! ah, where is all the help of our false friends? Where are the fair promises of our false friends? How have they deserted us, how have they utterly forgotten us! Oh, have pity on us, some little pity; at least you our best beloved friends! What services have we not rendered you, and how are we now repaid. Oh that we should not have warded off these sufferings when we could have done so with things so trifling! Is not the least torment here greater, much greater, indeed, than any torment ever was on earth? One hour in Purgatory lasts a hundred years. Lo! now we boil, now we burn, now we shriek aloud for help; but, more than all it is our misfortune to be deprived so long of the joy of His countenance; this it is that cuts through the heart, the sense, the soul!—And thus I expire.

*The Servant.*—O Eternal Wisdom, how hast Thou forsaken me! O God, how has death all at once become present before me! Alas, thou soul of mine, art thou still in my body? Lord of Heaven, do I still live? Ah, Lord, now will I praise Thee, and vow reformation to Thee till death. Oh, how very terrified I am! I did not think death was so near me. Truly, Lord, this sight shall not fail to profit me; every day I will be on the watch for death, and will look about me that he take me not by surprise. I will learn how to die; I will turn my thoughts to yonder world. Lord, I see that there is no remaining here; Lord, in sooth, I will not save up my sorrow and repentance till death. Oh, how terrified I am at this spectacle, I marvel that my soul is still in my body! Begone, begone, from me, soft reclining, long sleeping, good eating and drinking, perishable honours, delicateness and luxury! If but a little suffering here is so painful to me, how shall I ever endure immeasurable agony? O God, if indeed I were now to die thus, how would it be with me? What a load have I not still upon me! Lord, this very day I will set a poor man* to pray for my poor soul, and since all her friends have forsaken her I will befriend her.

---

\* According to a practice of the middle ages.

*Eternal Wisdom.*—See; this shouldst thou diligently look to whilst thou art in thy youth, and whilst thou hast still time to make things better. But when, in truth, thou hast reached this hour, and thou canst not make things better, then shouldst thou look at nothing on earth, except My death and My infinite mercy; so that Thy trust may repose wholly in Me.

*The Servant.*— O Lord, I prostrate myself at Thy feet, and I beseech Thee with bitter tears to chastise me here as Thou wilt, only keep it not in store for me in the next world. Woe is me, Lord, the fire of Purgatory and its unspeakable torments, how could I ever be so foolish as to think lightly of them, and how do I now stand in such great fear of them!

*Eternal Wisdom.*—Be of good heart, this thy fear is the beginning of wisdom, and a path to salvation. Or hast thou forgotten how all the Scriptures declare what great salvation is contained in the fear and diligent contemplation of death? Thou shouldst always praise God, for not to one in a thousand has it been granted to know Him, as to thee. Listen to a lamentable thing: they hear it spoken of; they know of it beforehand, and yet they allow it to pass by, and heed it not till they be swallowed up by it, and then they howl and weep when it is too late. Open thy eyes, count upon thy fingers, see how many of them have died around thee in thy own times; talk with them a little in thy heart; join thy old man to them as though it were dead; question them together; see with what fathomless sighs, with what bitter tears they will say: Oh, blessed is he that ever he was born, who follows sweet counsel and, in the misfortunes of others, learns wisdom! Prepare thyself well for thy departure hence; for truly thou sittest as a bird on the bough, and art as a man who stands on the water's edge, and looks at the swift sailing ship in which he will presently take his seat, and sail away for a strange land whence he will never more return. Therefore, so regulate thy life that when the ship comes for thee thou mayest be ready, and mayest joyfully take thy departure hence.

## 2

## HOW ONE SHOULD LIVE AN INTERIOR AND GODLY LIFE

*The Servant.*—Lord, many are the rules, many the ways of a godly life, the one is so, the other so. Many and various are the ways. Lord, the Scriptures are inexhaustible, their precepts innumerable. Teach me, O Eternal Wisdom, in a few words, out of the abyss of all the things they contain, to what I ought chiefly to hold fast in the way of a truly pious life.

*Eternal Wisdom.*—The truest, most useful, and most practical doctrine for thee in all the Scriptures that, in a few words, will more than amply convince thee of all the truth requisite for the attainment of the summit of perfection in a godly life, is this doctrine: Keep thyself secluded from all mankind, keep thyself free from the influence of all external things, disenthrall thyself from all that depends on chance or accident, and direct thy mind at all times on high in secret and divine contemplation, wherein, with a steady gaze from which thou never swervest, thou hast Me before thy eyes. And as to other exercises, such as poverty, fasting, watching, and every other castigation, bend them all to this as to their end, and use just so much and so many of them as may advance thee to it. Behold, thus wilt thou attain to the loftiest pitch of perfection, that not one person in a thousand comprehends, because, with their end in view, they all continue in other exercises, and so go astray the long years.

*The Servant.*—Lord, who can exist in the unswerving gaze of Thy divine vision at all times?

*Eternal Wisdom.*—No one who lives here below in this temporal scene. This has been said to thee only that thou mightest know at what thou shouldst aim, after what thou shouldst strive, to what thou shouldst turn thy heart and mind. And if ever thou losest sight of it, let it be to thee as if thy eternal salvation were taken away from thee; and do thou speedily turn to it again, so that thou mayest again obtain possession of it; and then must thou look carefully to thyself, for, if it escape from thee, thou art like a sailor from whose grasp the oars in a strong swell have slipped, and who does not know whither he shall direct his course. But if thou mayest not as yet have a constant abiding place in divine contemplation, let the perpetually repeated collecting of thy wandering thoughts, and the assiduous withdrawing of thyself to engage in it, procure thee constancy so far as it is possible. Listen, listen, My child, to the faithful instructions of thy faithful Father. O give heed to them! Shut them up in the bottom of thy heart; think Who it is that teaches thee all this, and how very much in earnest He is. Dost thou wish to become ever more and more faithful? Then set My precepts before thy eyes. Wherever thou sittest, standest, or walkest, think that I am present to thee, and that I either admonish or converse with thee. O, My child, keep within thyself keep thyself pure, disengaged, and retired. See, in this way wilt thou become conscious of My words; that good, too, will be made known to thee which, as yet, is greatly hidden from thee.

*The Servant.*—O, Eternal Wisdom, praised be Thou for ever! Ah, my Lord and most faithful friend, if I would not do it otherwise, Thou wouldst yet force me to do it with Thy sweet words and Thy gentle teaching. Lord, I ought and will do my very best towards it.

## 3
# HOW WE OUGHT LOVINGLY TO RECEIVE GOD

*The Servant.*—Eternal Wisdom, if my soul could only penetrate the heavenly shrine of Thy divine mysteries, I would question Thee further about love. And this would be my question: Lord, Thou hast so entirely poured out the abyss of Thy divine love in Thy Passion, that I wonder if Thou canst show any more signs of Thy love?

*Eternal Wisdom.*—Yes. Even as the stars of heaven are countless, so the love-tokens of My unfathomable love are uncounted.

*The Servant.*—Ah, sweet Love of mine! ah, tender Lord elect! how my soul languishes for Thy love! Turn Thy mild countenance towards me, outcast creature that I am; see how everything vanishes and passes away in me except only the one treasure of Thy ardent love, and therefore tell me something further of this rich and hidden treasure. Lord, Thou knowest well that it is love's right never to be satisfied with what concerns the Beloved; that the more it has the more it desires, how unworthy soever it may acknowledge itself to be, for such is the effect of the omnipotent power of love. O, beautiful Wisdom, now tell me the greatest and dearest mark of Thy love that in Thy adopted human nature Thou didst ever manifest, without taking into account the unfathomable love-token of Thy bitter death.

*Eternal Wisdom.*—Answer Me now a question. What is that of all lovely things which is most agreeable to a loving heart?

*The Servant.*—Lord, to my understanding nothing is so agreeable to a loving heart as the beloved Himself and His sweet presence.

*Eternal Wisdom.*—Even so. See, and on this account, that nothing which belongs to true love might be wanting to those who love Me, did My unfathomable love, as soon as I had resolved to depart by death out of this world to My Father, compel Me to give Myself and My loving presence at the table of the last supper to My dear disciples, and in all future times to My elect, because I knew beforehand the misery which many a languishing heart would suffer for My sake.

*The Servant.*—Oh, dearest Lord, and art Thou Thyself, Thy very Self, really here?

*Eternal Wisdom.*—Thou hast Me in the sacrament, before thee and with thee, as truly and really God and Man, according to soul and body, with flesh and blood, as truly as My pure Mother carried Me in her arms, and as truly as I am in heaven in My perfect glory.

*The Servant.*—Ah, gentle Wisdom, there is yet something in My heart, may I be allowed to utter it to Thee? Lord, it does not proceed from unbelief, I believe that what Thou willest Thou canst do; but, tender Lord, it is a marvel to me (if I may venture to say so) how the beautiful, the delightful and glorified body of my Lord in all its greatness, in all its divinity, can thus essentially conceal itself under the little shape of the bread which, relatively considered, is so out of all relation. Gentle Lord, be not angry with me on this account, for, as Thou art my Wisdom elect, I should be glad by Thy favour to hear something on this head out of Thy sweet mouth.

*Eternal Wisdom.*—In what manner My glorified body and My soul, according to the whole truth, are in the Sacrament, this can no tongue express, nor any mind conceive, for it is a work of My omnipotence. Therefore oughtest thou to believe it in all simplicity, and not pry much into it. And yet I must say a little to thee about it. I will thrust this wonder aside for thee with another wonder. Tell Me how it can be in nature that a great house should shape itself in a small mirror, or in every fragment of a mirror, when the mirror is broken? Or, how can this be, that the vast heavens should compress themselves into so small a space as thy small eye, the two being so very unequal to each other in greatness?

*The Servant.*—Truly, Lord, I cannot tell, it is a strange thing, for my eye is to the heavens but as a small point.

*Eternal Wisdom.*—Behold, though neither thy eye nor anything else in nature is equal to the heavens, and yet nature can do this thing, why should not I, the Lord of nature, be able to do many more things above nature? But now, tell me further, is it not just as great a miracle to create heaven and earth, and all creatures out of nothing, as to change bread invisibly into My body?

*The Servant.*—Lord, it is just as possible for Thee, so far as I can understand, to change something into something, as to create something out of nothing.

*Eternal Wisdom.*—Dost thou wonder then at that, and not at this? Tell Me further, thou believest that I fed five thousand persons with five loaves, where was the hidden matter which obeyed My words?

*The Servant.*—Lord, I know not.

*Eternal Wisdom.*—Or dost thou believe thou hast a soul?

*The Servant.*—This I do not believe, because I know it, for otherwise I should not be alive.

*Eternal Wisdom.*—And yet thou canst not see thy soul with thy bodily eyes.

*The Servant.*—Lord, I know that there are many more beings invisible to human eyes than such as we can see.

*Eternal Wisdom.*—Now listen: many a person there is of senses so gross as hardly to believe that anything which he cannot perceive with his senses really exists, concerning which the learned know that it is false. In like manner does the human understanding stand related to divine knowledge. Had I asked thee how the portals of the abyss are constructed, or how the waters in the firmament are held together, thou wouldst perhaps have answered thus: It is a question too deep for me, I cannot go into it: I never descended into the abyss, nor ever mounted up to the firmament. Well, I have only asked thee about earthly things which thou seest and hearest, and understandest not. Why shouldst thou wish, then, to understand what surpasses all the earth, all the heavens, and all the senses? Or why wilt thou needs inquire into it? Behold, all such wondering and prying thoughts proceed alone from grossness of sense, which takes divine and supernatural things after the likeness of things earthly and natural, and such is not the case. If a woman were to give birth to a child in a dark tower, and it were to be brought up there, and its mother were to tell it of the sun and the stars, the child would marvel greatly, and would think it all against reason and incredible, which its mother, nevertheless, knows so well to be true.

*The Servant.*—Indeed, Lord, I have nothing more to say, for Thou hast so enlightened my faith that I ought never to think of marvelling in my heart again, or why should I seek to enquire into the highest, who cannot comprehend the lowest? Thou art the truth which cannot lie; Thou art the highest wisdom that can do all things; Thou art the omnipotent who can dispose of all things. Oh, noble and loving Lord, I have often desired in my heart that, like holy Simeon in the temple, I might have received Thee bodily in my arms, might have pressed Thee to my heart and soul, so that the spiritual kiss of Thy presence might have been as truly mine as it was his. But now, Lord, I see that I receive Thee as truly as he, and so much the more nobly as Thy tender body is now glorified, and impassible, which then was passible. Wherefore, dearest Lord, if my heart had the love of all hearts, my conscience the purity of all the angels, and my soul the beauty of all souls so that by Thy grace I should be worthy of Thee, I would fain receive Thee to-day so affectionately, and so bury and sink Thee in the bottom of my heart and soul, that neither joy nor sorrow, neither life nor death, could separate Thee from me. Ah, sweet Lord, hadst Thou, my chosen love, only sent me Thy messenger, I should not have known, for all this world, how I ought to offer him a sufficient welcome. How then ought I to behave myself towards Him whom my soul loveth? Truly art Thou the only one thing in which everything is included, that, in time and eternity, my heart can desire. Or is there any thing else that my soul can desire with Thee that Thou art not? I will say nothing of that which is contrary to Thee, or which is without Thee, for that would be repugnant to me. Truly art Thou the comeliest of all to the eyes, the sweetest of all to the mouth, the tenderest of all to the touch, the most beloved of all to the heart! Lord, my soul neither sees nor hears, nor feels aught of all that is here below, but she finds it severally a thousand times lovelier in Thee my chosen love. Ah, Eternal Lord, how am I to restrain myself in Thy regard from wonder and delight? Thy presence inflames me, but Thy greatness terrifies me. My reason will needs do honour to its Lord, but my heart desires to love its only good, and lovingly to embrace it. Thou art my Lord and my God, but Thou art also my

Brother, and, if I may venture to say so, my beloved Spouse. Oh, what love, what rapture, and what great joy, what dignity do I not possess in Thee alone! Ah, sweet Lord, methinks that had I only been vouchsafed the grace to receive out of Thy open wounds, from Thy heart, one single drop of blood into my mouth, if I could have had my desire, it would have given me the fulness of joy. Ah, heartfelt, inconceivable wonder, now I have not only received from Thy heart or Thy hands, from Thy feet or Thy tender wounds, I have not only received one or two drops, but I have received all Thy hot, rose-coloured blood through my mouth into my heart and soul. Is not this a great thing? Ought I not to appreciate this which to the exalted angels is precious? Lord, would that all my limbs, and all that I am, were transformed into an unfathomable love for the sake of this sign of Thy love. Lord, what is there else in all this world that could rejoice my heart, or that it could desire, when Thou givest Thyself thus cordially to me to enjoy and love! Truly is it called a SACRAMENT OF LOVE. When was there anything lovelier seen or heard of than to embrace love itself; than to be changed by grace into love itself? Lord, I see no difference except that Simeon received Thee visibly, and I receive Thee invisibly. But as little as my bodily eyes can see Thy true humanity, just as little could his bodily eyes contemplate Thy divinity, except through faith, as I do now. Lord, what new power is lodged in this bodily sight? He whose spiritual eyes are opened, has not much to see with his bodily eyes, for the eyes of the spirit see far more really and truly. Lord, I know by faith, so far as one can know it, that I have Thee here; what do I wish for more? Lord, it is a thousand times better for me that I am unable to see Thee; how could I ever have the heart thus visibly to partake of Thee! As it is, that which is lovely and delightful remains, while that which is inhuman falls away. Lord, when I truly reflect how inscrutably well, how lovingly and wisely Thou hast regulated all things, my heart with a loud voice, exclaims: Oh, the great treasure of the abyss of Divine Wisdom, what must Thou not be in Thyself, if Thou art so much in Thy fair emanations! Now, O glorious Lord, look at the great and sincere desire of my heart. Lord, never was king or emperor so worthily received, never dear strange guest so cordially embraced, never bride so beautifully and tenderly taken home, nor so honourably maintained, as my soul desires to receive Thee, my most honoured emperor, my soul's most lovely Bridegroom, this day, and to introduce Thee to the innermost and the very best that my heart and soul are able to afford, and to offer it Thee as worthily as ever it was offered Thee by any creature. Wherefore, Lord, teach me how I should behave myself towards Thee, how, with due honour and love, I should receive Thee.

*Eternal Wisdom.*—Thou shouldst receive Me worthily, thou shouldst partake of Me with humility, thou shouldst keep Me earnestly, thou shouldst embrace Me with conjugal love, and have Me in My godly dignity before thy eyes. Spiritual hunger and actual devotion must impel thee to Me more than custom. The soul that wishes to feel Me interiorly in the recesses of a secluded life, and sweetly to enjoy Me, must, first of all, be cleansed from sin, must be adorned with virtue, encircled with self-denial, decked out with the red roses of ardent love, strewn over with the fair violets of humble submission, and the white lilies of perfect purity. She should pray to Me with peace of heart, for in peace is My dwelling-place. She should clasp Me in her arms to the exclusion of all strange affections; for these I avoid, and flee as the free bird avoids and flees the cage. She should sing Me the song of Sion, which is a song of fervent, loving, and measureless praise; then will I embrace her, and she shall incline herself on My breast. There, if she finds a calm repose, a pure vision, unusual fruition, a foretaste of eternal bliss, let her preserve it, let her keep it for herself, and, with a sighing heart, let her speak as follows: Truly art thou the hidden God, the secret good which no one can know that has not felt it.

*The Servant.*—Alas, the great blindness in which I have hitherto lived! I have plucked the red roses and have not smelt them; I have wandered among the blooming flowers and have not seen them; I have been as a dry branch amid the fresh dews of May. Never, O never can I sufficiently repent Thy having been for many a day so near me, and my having been so far from Thee. O, Thou sweet guest of pure souls, what a sorry welcome have I hitherto given Thee, what an ill return have I so frequently made Thee! How little desirous have I not shown myself of the sweet bread of angels! I had the precious balsam in my mouth, and felt it not. Ah, Thou delight of all angelic eyes, never as yet did I feel true delight in Thee! If it were announced to me that a bodily friend would visit me in the morning should I not rejoice at it all the night before? And yet, never did I prepare myself for the reception of Thee, as in reason I ought, Thou worthy guest, whom heaven and earth equally honour. Alas! how have I been wont to turn quickly away from Thee, how to drive Thee out of Thy own! O Eternal God, Thou even Thou Thyself, art here so truly present, and the angelic host is here, and yet I have approached so shyly and sluggishly. Of Thee I will say nothing; but, truly, Lord, I know of no spot within many miles, whither, if I had known for certain of the presence of blessed angels, those high and noble guests who at all times behold Thee, I should not have repaired of my own accord, and even if I had not seen them, still my heart, on their account, would have leapt in my body for joy. O sweet Lord and God, that Thou Thyself, the Lord of all angels, shouldst have been present here, and shouldst have had with Thee so many angelic choirs, and that I should not have given more heed to the place; this, this must ever be a sore affliction for me! I ought, at all events, to have approached the place where I knew Thee to be thus present, even though nothing else might have come of it. O God, how often have I stood distracted and without devotion on the very spot where Thou wast before me, and with me in the Blessed Sacrament; my body indeed stood there, but my heart was elsewhere. How often have I thought so little of Thee in Thy presence, that my heart has not even offered Thee an affectionate salutation, with a devout inclination. Gentle Lord, my eyes ought to have looked at Thee with joyous delight, my heart ought to have loved Thee with the fulness of desire, my mouth ought to have praised Thee with heartfelt, fervent jubilee; all my strength ought to have melted in Thy glad service. What did not Thy servant David do who leapt so joyously with all his might before the ark, in which there was nothing but corporal bread of heaven, nothing but corporal things! Lord, now do I stand here before Thee, and before all Thy angels, and with bitter tears fall at Thy feet. Remember, O, remember, tender Lord, that here, before me, Thou art my flesh and my brother, and forego Thy displeasure. O, forgive me all the dishonour that ever I offered Thee, for I am sorry for it, and must ever be sorry for it; for the light of Thy wisdom begins only now to enlighten me; and the place where Thou art, not only according to Thy divinity, but according to Thy humanity, shall be honoured by me evermore. Ah, Thou sweetest good, Thou worthy Lord and lovely guest of my soul, another question would I gladly ask: Tell me, gentle Lord, what is it Thou givest Thy beloved with Thy real presence in the Sacrament, provided she receives Thee with love and desire?

*Eternal Wisdom.*—Is that a fitting question for a lover? What have I better than Myself? He who possesses the object of his love, what else has he to ask for? He who gives himself, what has he refused? I give Myself to thee, and take thee from thyself, and unite thee to Me. Thou loseth thyself, and art wholly transformed into Me. What does the sun in his brightest reflection bestow on the unclouded sky? Yes, what does the bright star of the morning dawn bestow on the dark night? Or what do the fair and ravishing adornments of summer bestow after the cold, wintry, melancholy season?

*The Servant.*—O Lord, they bestow precious gifts.

*Eternal Wisdom.*—They seem precious to thee because they are visible to thee. Behold, the smallest gift that flows from Me in the Blessed Sacrament reflects more splendour in eternity than any sunny brightness; it sheds more light than any morning star; it adorns thee more ravishingly in eternal beauty than ever did any adornment of summer the earth. Or is not My bright divinity more radiant than any sun, My noble soul more resplendent than any star, My glorified body more ravishing than any ravishment of summer? And yet all these things hast thou truly received here.

*The Servant.*—O Lord, why then are they not more sensibly felt? Lord, I often approach in such dryness that all light, all grace and sweetness are as strange to me, methinks, as to a man born blind, who never saw the sun. Lord, if I may venture to say so, I could indeed wish that, in Thy real presence, Thou hadst given testimony of Thyself.

*Eternal Wisdom.*—The less the testimony, the purer thy faith and the greater thy reward. The Lord of nature operates with such secrecy a blessed increase in many a fair tree, that no eye nor other sense can perceive it till it is accomplished. Now, I am not an exteriorly working good, but an interiorly shining light; an interiorly working good which is so much the nobler as it is the more spiritual.

*The Servant.*—Alas! how few men there are who perceive this, who weigh thoroughly what they receive. They draw near like the rest generally, in an ill and inconsiderate manner, and, therefore, as they go up empty, they come away without grace. They do not ruminate their food so as to ponder what they have received.

*Eternal Wisdom.*—To the well prepared I am the bread of eternal life, to the little prepared the bread of dryness, but to the unprepared I am a deadly blow, an eternal curse.

*The Servant.*—O Lord, what a terrible thing is this! Lord, whom dost Thou call the well prepared, the little prepared, and the unprepared?

*Eternal Wisdom.*—The well prepared are the purified, the little prepared such as cleave to temporal things, but the unprepared are the sinful who continue by will and by deed in mortal sin.

*The Servant.*—But, tender Lord, if at the time a person is heartily sorry for his sins, and strives, to the best of his ability, to rid himself wholly of them, conformably to Christian precept, how is it then with him?

*Eternal Wisdom.*—In such a case a man is, for the time, no longer in sin.

*The Servant.*—Lord, in my opinion, it were one of the greatest things this world could accomplish, if any person, while living in this temporal state, was able to prepare himself worthily enough for Thy reception.

*Eternal Wisdom.*—That person was never yet born; nay, if a man had the native purity of all the angels, the sanctity of all the saints, and the good works of all mankind, he would yet be unworthy.

*The Servant.*—Ah, beloved Lord, with what trembling hearts ought not persons so unworthy, so deprived of grace, as we are, to approach Thee.

*Eternal Wisdom.*—If a man only does his best, nothing more is required of him, for God completes what is left incomplete. A sick man should cast aside all reserve, and should approach the physician whose attendance is his cure.

*The Servant.*—Lord, beloved Lord, which is better, OFTEN, or SELDOM, to receive Thee in the Blessed Sacrament?

*Eternal Wisdom.*—For him whose grace and devotion perceptibly increase by it, to receive Me often is profitable.

*The Servant.*— But, Lord, if a man in his own opinion remains the same, and cannot prove that he either increases or decreases by it in holiness, or if he is often visited by spiritual dryness, how should he then behave himself?

*Eternal Wisdom.*—A man, provided only he does his part, should not withdraw himself because of spiritual dryness. For the salvation of that soul which by God's will suffers from spiritual dryness is often accomplished as nobly in the light of pure faith alone, as in great sweetness. I am a boon which, turned to account, increases, but which, saved up, wastes away. It is better to approach once a week with a deep sense of real humility, than once a year with an overweening self-approbation.

*The Servant.*—Lord, at what time does the influence of grace from the Blessed Sacrament take place?

*Eternal Wisdom.*—In the very moment of actual reception.

*The Servant.*—Lord, but what if a man have a fervent desire for Thy bodily presence in the Sacrament, and he must yet be deprived of it?

*Eternal Wisdom.*—Many a man after being filled with Me, goes away hungry, and many a man obtains Me, though the table be empty; the former merely receives Me bodily, the latter enjoys Me spiritually.

*The Servant.*—Lord, has that man any advantage who receives Thee bodily and spiritually, over him who only receives Thee spiritually?

*Eternal Wisdom.*—Tell me whether that man has more who has Me and My grace, or he who has only My grace alone?

*The Servant.*—Lord, how long dost Thou remain in Thy real presence with a man who has received Thee?

*Eternal Wisdom.*—As long as the image and likeness of the Sacrament remain.

## 4
## A PRAYER TO BE SAID WHEN THOU GOEST TO RECEIVE OUR LORD'S HOLY BODY

O Thou living fruit, Thou sweet blossom, Thou delicious paradise apple of the blooming fatherly heart, Thou sweet vine of Cyprus in the vineyard of Engaddi, who will give me to receive Thee so worthily this day that Thou shalt desire to come to me, to dwell with me, and never to separate from me! O unfathomable good, that fillest heaven and earth, incline Thyself graciously this day, and despise not Thy poor creature. Lord, if I am not worthy of Thee, yet do I stand in need of Thee. Ah, gentle Lord, art Thou not He who with one word created heaven and earth? Lord, with one word canst Thou restore health to my sick soul. O Lord, do unto me according to Thy grace, according to Thy infinite mercy, and not according to my deserts. Yes,

Thou art the innocent Paschal Lamb, which at this day is still offered up for the sins of all mankind. Ah, Thou sweet-tasting bread of heaven, which contains all sweet tastes according to the desire of everyone's heart, make the hungry mouth of my soul to rejoice in Thee this day; give me to eat and to drink; strengthen, adorn, and unite me interiorly to Thee. Ah, Eternal Wisdom, come down so powerfully this day into my soul, that all my enemies may be driven out of her, all my crimes be melted away, and all my sins be forgiven. Enlighten my understanding with the light of true faith. Inflame my will with Thy sweet love. Cheer up my mind with Thy glad presence, and give virtue and perfection to all my powers. Watch over me at my death, that I may enjoy Thy beatific vision in eternal bliss. Amen.

## 5
## HOW WE SHOULD AT ALL TIMES PRAISE GOD

*The Servant.*—"*Praise the Lord, O my soul, in my life I will praise the Lord; I will sing to my God as long as I shall be.*" *

Who will grant, O God, to my full heart to fulfill before my death its desire for Thy praise? Who will grant me worthily to praise, in my day, the beloved Lord whom my soul loveth? Ah, tender Lord, would that there issued from my heart as many sweet tones as ever have issued from sweet harpings, as many as there are leaves and blades of grass, would that they were all addressed on high to Thee in Thy heavenly court, so that a song of such a delightful and unheard-of praise might burst from my heart, as would be

---
* Psalm cxiv. i.

pleasing to the eyes of my Lord, and full of joy to all the heavenly host! Ah, beloved Lord, although I am not worthy to praise Thee, still my soul desires that the heavens should praise Thee, when, in their ravishing beauty and sublime splendour they are lit up with the multitude of glittering stars; and the fair delightful meadow, when, in all the bliss of summer it glistens afresh in blithesome beauty, in manifold flowery adornment; and all the sweet thoughts and fervent desires that ever a pure and affectionate heart conceived for Thee when it was encompassed by the refreshing summer-delights of Thy illuminating Spirit. Lord, when I but think of Thy high praise, my heart is ready to melt in my breast, my thoughts wander from me, speech fails me, and all knowledge escapes me. Something shines in my heart beyond the power of words, when I will needs praise Thee, O infinite Good; for, if I take the fairest creatures, the most exalted spirits, the purest beings, Thou yet surpassest them all unspeakably. If I enter the deep abyss of Thy goodness, there all praise disappears in its own littleness. Lord, when I behold living forms of beauty, creatures gentle and engaging, they say to my heart: Oh, see how right gracious He is from whom we emanate, from whom all that is beautiful has issued! If I traverse heaven and earth, the universe and the abyss, wood and grove, mountain and valley, lo! they one and all fill my ears with a rich canticle of Thy unfathomable praise. Then, when I mark with what infinite beauty and harmony Thou orderest all things, both evil and good, I am dumb and speechless. But, Lord, when I remember that Thou Thyself art this praiseworthy good which my soul has chosen out solely for herself, as her one only and undivided love, my heart, for praise, is like to burst within me, and to cease its throbbings. Oh, tender Lord, have regard, therefore, for the great and ardent desire of my heart and soul, and teach me how to praise Thee worthily, and how to serve Thee acceptably before I depart hence, for this is what my soul thirsts after in my body.

*Eternal Wisdom.*—Wouldst thou then gladly praise Me?

*The Servant.*—Alas! Lord, why dost Thou provoke me? Thou knowest all hearts, Thou knowest that my heart is ready to turn round in my body from the true desire of Thy praise, which from my childhood's day till now I have had.

*Eternal Wisdom.*—*Praise becometh the upright.*\*

*The Servant.*—Alas! my Lord all my uprightness lies in Thy boundless compassion. Beloved Lord, the frogs praise Thee in the pool, and if they cannot speak, yet do they croak. Full well do

---

\* Psalm xxxii. i.

I know who I am. Lord, I know that rather than praise Thee, I ought to lament and beg pardon for my sins. And yet, O unfathomable good, scorn not the desire I have to praise Thee, miserable worm that I am. Lord, though the cherubim and seraphim, and the countless number of all exalted spirits, praise Thee according to their utmost powers, yet what can they do more as regards Thy infinite dignity, far removed above all praise, than the very least of Thy creatures? Lord, Thou standest in need of no creature's praise; but Thy infinite goodness is made all the more manifest the more Thou givest Thyself to the praise of those who are without desert.

*Eternal Wisdom.*—Whoever thinks he can praise Me to the fulness of My worth, acts like him who chases the wind and trys to grasp a shadow. And yet it is permitted to thee and all creatures to praise Me according to your ability; for there never was a creature so little, nor so great, nor so good, nor so wicked, neither will there be one, but it either praises Me or testifies to My praise; and the more it is united with Me, the more praiseworthy it finds Me; and the more thy praise is like the praise of eternal glory, the more praiseworthy it is to Me; and the more this praise of thine is abstracted in imagination from all creatures and united in true devotion to Me, the more it is like the praise of eternal glory. A fervent contemplating sounds better in My ears than merely a praising with words, and a heartfelt sighing sounds better than a lofty appeal. A total subjection of one's self under God and all mankind, in the wish to be as nothing in their sight, is a sound for Me above all sweet sounds. I Myself never appeared on earth so worthy of praise before My Father as when I hung in mortal agony on the cross. Some persons praise Me with fair words, but their hearts are far from Me, and of such praise I make no account. So likewise, some persons praise Me when things go according to their desires, but when things begin to go wrong with them, their praise ceases, and such praise is disagreeable to Me. But that praise is good and precious in My divine eyes when, with thy heart, thy words and works, thou dost praise me as fervently in sorrow as in joy, in utter adversity as in full prosperity; for then thou thinkest of Me and not of thyself.

*The Servant.*—Lord, I desire not sufferings from Thee, neither will I give cause for such things; but I will give myself up wholly and entirely, according to the desire of my heart, to Thy eternal praise, whereas, before, I never could truly forsake and utterly forget myself. Lord, if Thou wert to permit me to become the most despised person the whole earth could produce, Lord, even this I would suffer for the sake of Thy praise. Lord, I yield myself up this day to Thy grace and mercy; nay, if I were to be accused of the foulest murder that ever any man committed, so that whoever saw me should spit in my face, Lord, I would willingly bear it in praise of Thee, provided I only stood guiltless in Thy sight. But even if I were guilty, I would still endure it in praise of Thy blessed justice, which is a thousand times more precious to me than my own honour. For every term of reproach cast at me I would give Thee a particular praise, and with the good thief would say to Thee: *Lord, I receive the due reward of my deeds, but what hast Thou done amiss? Lord, remember me, when Thou comest into Thy Kingdom!* And should it be Thy will to take me now from hence, if it were for Thy praise, I would not look about me for a respite, but I would desire to be taken hence; and I would desire that, if it should have been my lot to have become as old even as Mathusala, every year of the long period, and every week of the years, and every day of the weeks, and every hour of the days, and every minute of the hours, might praise Thee for me in such rapturous praise as never did any saint in the veritable bright reflection of the saints, and this as many times as the grains of dust are countless in the sunshine, and that they might fulfill this my good desire, as though I myself had all the time lived to fulfill it. Therefore,

Lord, take me early or late to Thyself, for such is my heart's desire. Lord, I will say still more, that, if I had now to depart hence, and it were to Thy praise that I should burn fifty years in purgatory, I am ready to incline myself at Thy feet, and gladly accept it all to Thy eternal praise; blessed be the fire of purgatory in which Thy praise is fulfilled in me! Lord, Thou, and not myself, art what I here love and here seek. Lord, Thou comprehendest all things, Thou knowest all hearts, Thou knowest that these are my unshaken sentiments; nay, if I knew that I should have to lie for ever at the bottom of hell, however it might afflict my heart to be robbed of Thy ravishing vision, I yet would not cease from Thy praise; and could I retrieve the lost time of all men, reform their misdeeds, and by means of praise and honour, make full amends for all the dishonour that ever was shown Thee, I would willingly do it; and if it were indeed possible, then, from the lowest abyss of hell must needs burst forth from me a beautiful song of praise which would penetrate hell, the earth, air, and all the heavens, till it arrived before Thy divine countenance. But, if this were not possible, I would yet wish to praise Thee here all the more, that I might even here rejoice in Thee all the more. Lord, do with Thy poor creature what is for Thy praise; for let what will happen to me, so long as there is any breath in my mouth I will utter Thy praise; and when I lose my utterance, I desire that the raising of my finger may be a confirmation and conclusion of all the praise I ever spoke; nay, when my body falls to dust, I desire that, from every grain of dust, an infinite praise may pierce through the hard stones, through all the heavens up to Thy divine presence, till the last day, when body and soul shall again unite in Thy praise.

*Eternal Wisdom.*—In this desire and good intention thou shouldst remain till death—such praise is pleasing to Me.

*The Servant.*—Ah, sweet Lord, since Thou deignest and desirest to receive praise from me, poor sinful person that I am, it is my desire that Thou wouldst show me three things, namely, how, wherewith, and at what time I ought to praise Thee. Tell me, dearest Lord, is the external praise which is given by words and singing, any way profitable?

*Eternal Wisdom.*—It is certainly profitable, and especially as it stirs up the interior man, which it very often stirs up, above all in the case of newly converted persons.

*The Servant.*—Lord, I also am filled with the desire (seeing that one should be glad to begin in time, what one will have to practice in eternity) to attain the diligent praising of Thee in my interior, and that I should not be interrupted in Thy praise at any time, even for the space of a second. Lord, out of this very desire I have often spoken as follows: "O, thou firmament why dost thou hasten and revolve so fast? I beseech thee, stand still in this moment, until I shall have thoroughly praised my Lord according to my heart's desire. Lord, when perchance I have been a little while neglectful of Thy present praise, and have shortly come to myself, I have interiorly cried out as follows: O Lord, it is a thousand years that I have thought no more of my Beloved! O Lord, teach me, then, as much as Thou canst, while my soul is yet in my body, how I may attain to praise Thee continually and without relaxation.

*Eternal Wisdom.*—He who in all things is mindful of Me, who keeps himself from sin, and is diligent in virtue, praises Me at all times; but still, if thou wouldst seek after the highest sort of praise, listen to something more: The soul is like to a light peacock's feather; if nothing is attached to it, it is very easily borne aloft by its own mobility towards the sky, but if it is laden with anything it falls to the ground. In like manner, a mind that is purified from all heaviness of sin is also raised by virtue of its native nobility, with the help of gentle contemplation, to heavenly things; and therefore, when it happens that a mind is disengaged from all bodily desires, and is set interiorly at rest, so that its every thought cleaves at all times inseparably to the immutable Good, such a mind fulfills My praise at all times; for in the state of purity, so far as words can express it, man's carnal sense is so wholly drowned and so wholly transformed from earthiness into a spiritual and an angelic semblance, that, whatever he receives exteriorly, whatever he does or operates, whether he eats, drinks, sleeps, or wakes is nothing else but the very purest praise.

*The Servant.*—Ah, Lord, what a truly sweet doctrine is this! Lovely Wisdom, three things there are still that I should be glad to have explained. One is: Where shall I find the most reasons to praise Thee?

*Eternal Wisdom.*—In the first origin of all good, and then in its outflowing springs.

*The Servant.*—Lord, as to the origin, it is too high for me, too unknown to me; there let the tall cedars praise Thee, the heavenly spirits, the angelic minds. And yet will I too press forward like a rude thistle with my praise, that they may be admonished by the spectacle of my impotent longings of their own high worthiness, that they may be incited in their pure brightness to praise Thee, just as though the cuckoo were to give the nightingale occasion to sing a ravishing song. But the outflowings of Thy goodness; these will be proper for my praise. Lord, when I ponder well what I was formerly, how often Thou hast protected me, from what evil chains and bonds Thou hast delivered me, O Thou Everlasting Good, it is a wonder that my heart does not wholly melt in Thy praise! Lord, how long didst Thou not wait for me, how kindly didst Thou not receive me, how sweetly in secret didst Thou not anticipate me and interiorly warn me! How ungrateful soever I might sometimes be, still Thou didst not desist until Thou hadst drawn me to Thee. Ought I then not to praise Thee, my gentle Lord? Yes, truly do I desire that a rich praise should ascend before Thy eyes, even such a great and joyous praise as that rendered by the angels when they first beheld the sight of their own constancy and the reprobation of their fallen companions; as that uttered in the joy felt by the miserable souls in Purgatory when they come forth from their grim prison-house before Thee, and behold for the first time Thy countenance beaming with delight and love; a praise even as that unfathomable praise which will resound in the streets of the heavenly city after the last judgment, when the elect shall be separated in everlasting security from the wicked. Lord, one thing I should also like to know respecting Thy praise is this: How all that is naturally good in me may be referred to Thy everlasting praise?

*Eternal Wisdom.*—Inasmuch as nobody in this temporal state can be sure, from actual knowledge, of the true difference between nature and grace, so when anything gracious, joyous, or agreeable, arises in thy mind, whether it be from nature of from grace, enter quickly and speedily into thy interior, and make an oblation of it to God, so that it may be consumed in My praise, because I am the Lord of nature and grace, and in this way will nature now to thee become supernatural.

*The Servant.*—Lord, but how then shall I turn even the imaginations of evil spirits to Thy eternal praise?

*Eternal Wisdom.*—To the suggestions or inspirations of an evil spirit speak thou as follows: Lord, as often as this wicked spirit or any other sends me against my will such disagreeable thoughts, let me of my own premeditated will send Thee the most fervent praise in his stead, even the very praise which the same evil spirit ought to have given Thee throughout all eternity had he remained loyal, so that in his reprobate state I may represent his place in praising Thee; and as often as he inspires me with such odious thoughts, let my good praise ascend to Thee.

*The Servant.*—O Lord, now do I indeed see that to good men all things may be turned into good, when even the very worst things of the evil spirit can in such a way be made good things. But now tell me one thing more. Ah, Thou gracious

Lord, how am i to turn all that I hear, all that I see, to Thy praise and glory?

*Eternal Wisdom.*—As often as thou seest a great number of people, as often as thou beholdest an exceeding fair multitude, say from the very bottom of thy heart: Lord, as often and as beautifully must the thousand times a thousand angelic spirits who stand before Thee salute Thee lovingly this day in my name, and the ten thousand times a thousand spirits who serve Thee praise Thee to-day for me, and they must desire for me all the holy desires of the saints, and that the ravishing beauty of all creatures may do Thee honour to-day for me.

*The Servant.*—O my sweet Lord, how hast Thou not refreshed and increased my zeal in Thy praise! But truly, Lord, this temporal praise has stirred up my heart and alas! set my soul a longing for the praise which is everlasting and eternal. When, my own elected Wisdom, when will the bright day arise, when will the glad hour arrive of a perfectly prepared death and departure from this scene of wretchedness to my Beloved! Ah me, I begin so to languish, so ardently to long after my heart's only love! When, O when shall I ever possess it? How lingering is the time, how late it will be before I behold face to face the delight of my soul's eyes, before I enjoy Thee according to my heart's desire! O misery of banishment, what a misery thou art to him who considers himself banished in very truth! Behold, Lord, there is hardly any one on earth but has some friend to visit, some place on which to rest his foot a little while. Alas, my only one, Thou whom my soul alone seeks and desires, Thou knowest that I have no other refuge, than in Thee alone! Lord, whatever I hear and see, if I find Thee not, is a torment to me; the society of all mankind without Thee is bitterness to me. Lord, what should rejoice me, what detain me here?

*Eternal Wisdom.*—Here on earth shouldst thou often wander in the delightful orchard of My blooming praise. In this transient life there is no truer prelude to the celestial habitations than is to be found among those who praise God in the joy of a serene heart. There is nothing that cheers a man's mind so much, and lightens his sufferings; that drives away evil spirits, and makes sadness disappear, as joyous praising of God. God is near those who praise Him; the angels are familiar with them: they are profitable to themselves; it betters their neighbour and gladdens the soul; all the heavenly host is honoured by cheerful minded praise.

*The Servant.*—Sweet Lord, my tender, my Eternal Wisdom! I desire that when my eyes first awaken in the morning, my heart may awaken too, and that there may burst from it a high-flaming fiery love-torch of Thy praise, with the most fervent love of the most loving heart that exists in time, according to the most ardent love of the most exalted seraphim in eternity, in the fathomless love with which THOU, Heavenly Father, lovest Thy only Son, and with the most sweet love of the Holy Ghost who proceeds from Father and Son; and I desire that this praise may resound so sweetly in the Fatherly heart as never did yet the strings of all earthly instruments in a joyous mind; and that this love-torch may send up so sweet a savour of praise as though it were smoking incense composed of all precious herbs and spices of all virtues finely powdered together in their highest perfection; and lastly, that the sight of it may be so beautifully blooming in graces as never any May was known to be in its most ravishing bloom; so that it may be a delightful aspect for Thy divine eyes and all the heavenly host. All my desire is, that this love-torch may at all times blaze out fervently in my prayers, from my mouth in my singing, in my thoughts, words, and works, that it may subdue all my enemies, consume all my sins, and obtain for me a happy end, so that the end of this my temporal praise may be but the beginning of my everlasting, my eternal praise. Amen.

. . .

*Let everybody who desires to meditate briefly, properly, and earnestly on the Passion of our Lord Jesus Christ, in whom all our salvation lies, and who desires to be thankful for His manifold sufferings, learn by heart the hundred choice meditations which hereafter follow, severally, according to their sense, which is comprised in few words, and go over them devoutly every day, with a hundred venias or otherwise, as it may suit him best, and at every venia, when it relates to our Blessed Lady, let him say a Pater Noster, or an Ave Maria, or a Salve Regina, for in this manner were they revealed to a preacher by God, at a time when he stood before a crucifix after Matins, and fervently complained to God that he could not well meditate on His torments, and that it was so bitter a thing for him to meditate on them, inasmuch as; up to that hour, he had had herein great infirmity, from which he was then relieved. The prayers he afterwards appended, in a short form, so that all might be free to find matter for themselves to pray agreeably to their own feelings, but should the prayers prove too many for a person all at once, let him divide them into even daily hours, or into the seven days of the week, according as they are here noted down.*

# THE THIRD PART

## ONE HUNDRED MEDITATIONS AND PRAYERS, COMPRISED IN FEW WORDS.

# ON SUNDAY, OR AT MATINS

O Eternal Wisdom, my heart reminds Thee of Thy sorrow of soul. 1. When after the Last Supper on the Mount, Thou wast bathed in Thy bloody sweat because of the anxiety of Thy heart; 2. And when like an enemy Thou wast made prisoner, cruelly bound, and led miserably away; 3. When, Lord, Thou wast sacrilegiously maltreated in the night with hard blows, and with blindfolding of Thine eyes; 4. Early accused before Caiphas and pronounced worthy of death; 5. Seen by Thy affectionate mother with unspeakable sorrow of heart; 6. Thou wast ignominiously presented before Pilate, falsely accused, and condemned to die; 7. Thou, O Eternal Wisdom, wast mocked as a fool in a white garment before

Herod; 8. Thy fair body was torn and rent without mercy by the cruel whips of Thy scourgers; 9. Thy delicate head was pierced with sharp thorns and Thy sweet face, in consequence, drenched with blood; 10. Thus condemned Thou wast led miserably and shamefully with Thy cross to death.

Alas, my only hope, let me, therefore, remind Thee to give me Thy fatherly aid in all my distresses. Oh, unloose my sinful fetters, guard me against secret vice and open guilt, shelter me from the false councils of the enemy, and from the occasion of all crime, inspire me with a sincere sympathy for Thy own sufferings and for those of Thy tender mother. Lord, at my last departure, judge me mercifully, teach me to condemn worldly honours, and to serve Thee wisely. Let all my infirmities be healed in Thy wounds. Let my reason be fortified and adorned by the injuries inflicted on Thy head, and may Thy whole Passion be imitated by me according to my ability. Amen.

Sweet Lord! 1. When on the high branches of the cross Thy eyes were extinguished and turned in their sockets; 2. Thy divine ears filled with mockery and blasphemy; 3. Thy delicate nostrils stopped with rank smells; 4. Thy sweet mouth with bitter drink; 5. Thy tender feeling visited with rude blows. Therefore do I beg that Thou wouldst guard this day my eyes from all dissolute sights, my ears from voluptuous speech. Lord, take away from me all relish of bodily things, make all temporal things unpleasant to me, and rid me of all tenderness for my own body.

# ON MONDAY, OR AT PRIME

𝒜h, tender Lord! 1. When Thy divine head was bowed down by weakness and utter debility; 2. Thy fair throat very grievously distended; 3. Thy blessed features polluted with spittle and blood; 4. Thy clear complexion made livid; 5. All Thy beautiful form smitten with death. Grant me, therefore, O Lord, to love bodily pain, and to seek all my rest in Thee, to endure injuries willingly from others, to desire contempt, to die to my affections and all my lusts.

Sweet Lord! 1. When Thy right hand was nailed down; 2. Thy left hand struck through; 3. Thy right arm extended; 4. Thy left stretched out; 5. Thy right foot hammered through; 6. Thy left made fast; 7. Thou didst hang suspended in a swoon; 8. And in great weariness of Thy divine limbs; 9. All Thy tender joints were immovably strained on the hard bed of the cross; 10. Thy body was drenched in many places with Thy hot blood. Therefore, O Lord, I beseech that I may be made immovably fast to Thee in joy and sorrow, that all the powers of my body and soul may be distended on Thy cross, and my reason and affections nailed to it. Grant me inability to indulge in bodily pleasure, promptness in seeking Thy praise and honour. I crave that no limb of my body may be without a living token of Thy death, a spontaneous proof of the image of Thy Passion.

# ON TUESDAY, OR AT TIERCE

Tender Lord! 1. Thy blooming body pined and withered away on the cross; 2. Thy weary and tender back leant uneasily against the hard wood; 3. Thy heavy frame painfully gave way; 4. All Thy limbs were covered with sores; 5. Thy heart endured it lovingly. Lord, be Thy withering a re-blooming to me for ever. Thy uneasy leaning my spiritual rest. Thy giving way, my powerful support. All Thy wounds must heal mine, and Thy loving heart inflame mine with fervour.

Sweet Lord! 1. First in Thy mortal agony Thou wast mocked with scornful words; 2. And with contemptuous gestures; 3. Thou wast utterly annihilated in their hearts; 4. Thou didst continue under it steadfast; 5. And didst pray to Thy

Father for them lovingly; 6. Thou, the innocent Lamb, wast numbered with the guilty; 7. Thou wast condemned and reviled by the thief on Thy left; 8. But wast invoked by him on the right; 9. Thou forgavest the latter all his sins; 10. Thou didst unlock for him the gates of paradise.

Beloved Lord! teach me, Thy servant, to bear with firmness every ignominious word, every scornful gesture, and all sorts of contempt for Thy sake, and lovingly to excuse my enemies before Thee. Ah, Thou infinite good, behold, this day I offer up, before the eyes of Thy heavenly Father, Thy innocent death for my guilty life. Lord, with the thief I cry out to Thee: Remember me when Thou comest into Thy kingdom! Condemn me not for my evil deeds, forgive all my sins, undo for me the gates of the heavenly paradise!

## ON WEDNESDAY, OR AT SEXT

Tender Lord! 1. At that hour Thou wast forsaken for my sake of all men; 2. Thy friends had renounced Thee; 3. Thou stoodst naked and robbed of all honour and raiment; 4. Thy power then seemed overcome; 5. They treated Thee without mercy, and Thou didst bear it all in meekness and silence; 6. Alas, for Thy gentle heart, Thou who alone didst know at that time the depth of Thy Mother's sorrow of heart; 7. And didst see her deplorable state; 8. And didst hear her lamentable words; 9. And at Thy mortal separation didst commend her to the filial piety of Thy disciple; 10. And the disciple to her maternal love.

Oh therefore, Thou pattern of all virtues, take away from me all pernicious love of men, and all inordinate affection of friends; strip me of all impatience; give me steadfastness against all evil spirits, and meekness against all violent men. Give me, gentle Lord, Thy bitter death in the bottom of my heart, in my prayers, and in the practice of good works. O tender Lord, I commend myself this day to the true fidelity and care of Thy pure Mother and Thy beloved disciple.

[Here say a Salve Regina or an Ave Maria.]

O pure and tender Mother, I shall remind thee to-day of the infinite sorrow of heart which thou didst endure.—1. At the first aspect of thy dear Child when thou didst see Him suspended in agony; 2. Thou couldst not then come to Hiss assistance; 3. Thou didst gaze in anguish of heart at thy beloved Son expiring before thine eyes; 4. Thou didst lament over Him with great lamentation; 5. And He comforted thee very kindly; 6. His divine words pierced thy heart; 7. Thy lamentable gestures softened the hard hearts of the Jews; 8. Thy maternal arms and hands were most reverentially lifted up; 9. But thy sick body sank exhausted on the ground; 10. Where thy tender mouth did affectionately kiss His fallen blood.

Oh, then Mother of all graces, watch over me like a mother for my whole life, and graciously shield me in the hour of my death. O gentle Lady! behold, that is the hour for the sake of which I desire to be thy servant all my days. That is the dreadful hour which frightens my heart and soul, for then there will be an end to prayer and supplication. Then shall I, poor wretch, not know to whom to turn. Therefore, thou unfathomable abyss of divine compassion, I fall at thy feet this day with the fervent sighs of my heart, that I may then be found worthy of thy joyous presence. How should he ever despond, or what can injure him whom here, O purest Mother, thou dost protect? Ah, thou only consolation, defend me against the terrible looks of the wicked spirits, lend me aid and protection against the hands of the enemy! Hearken consolingly to my wretched sighs, look kindly with the eyes of thy compassion on my ghastly and enfeebled frame. Reach me thy beneficent hands. Receive my poor soul. With thy radiant countenance present it before the severe Judge, and install it in everlasting bliss!

# ON THURSDAY, OR AT NONE

*O* Thou most intimate delight of the Heavenly Father! 1. How wast Thou abandoned at that hour on the cross to every pang of bitter death exteriorly, and robbed of all sweetness and solace interiorly! 2. Thou didst utter a cry of misery to Thy Father; 3. Thy will Thou didst unite wholly to His; 4. Thou didst thirst bodily by reason of great dryness! 5. Thou didst thirst spiritually by reason of great love; 6. Thy thirst was bitterly quenched; 7. And when all things were fulfilled Thou didst exclaim: Consummatum est? 8. Thou wast obedient unto Thy Father, even unto death; 9. And Thou didst commend Thy Spirit into His Fatherly hands; 10. And then Thy noble soul separated from Thy body.

Ah, Thou loving Lord, in this Thy love I desire

that Thou wouldst open Thy Fatherly ears at all times to my call, and give me in all things a will united to Thine. Lord, quench in me all thirst after bodily things; make me thirst after spiritual goods. Sweet Lord, let Thy bitter drink change all my afflictions into sweetness. Grant me to persevere in perfect thoughts and in good works until death, and that I may never swerve from Thy obedience. Eternal Wisdom, let my spirit be transferred from this day forth into Thy hands, so that at its final departure it may be joyfully received by Thee. Lord, grant me a life pleasing in Thy sight; a death well prepared for; an end made sure by Thee. Lord, let Thy bitter death make amends for, and complete my insufficient works, so that at my last hours, guilt and punishment may be wholly effeced.

## ON FRIDAY, OR AT VESPERS

Ah, my Lord, remember, 1. How the sharp spear was thrust into Thy divine side; 2. How the purple blood ran out; 3. How the living water gushed forth; 4. And with what bitter toil Thou didst garner me up; 5. And how generously Thou didst ransom me; Loving Lord! may Thy deep wounds shelter me from all my enemies; Thy living water cleanse me from all my sins; Thy rose-coloured blood adorn me with all graces and virtues. Tender Lord! May the prize Thou didst so bitterly win bind me to Thee! The ransom Thou didst so freely pay unite me eternally with Thee. Oh, thou chosen consolation of all sinners, oh, thou sweet Queen, remember to-day. 1. How thou didst stand under the cross, and how, as thy Son hung dead above thee, thou didst cast on

Him many a look of misery; 2. How affectionately His arms were received by thee; 3. With what fidelity pressed to thy blood-stained face; 4. His bleeding wounds, His dead and ghastly features, were by thee kissed again and again; 5. How many a death-wound thy heart then received; 6. How many a fervent unfathomable sigh burst from thee; 7. How many scalding tears thou didst shed; 8. Thy miserable words were so full of sorrow; 9. Thy most gracious figure was so steeped in affliction; 10. Thy woeful heart was without consolation from all mankind. Oh, pure Lady, on this account forget not to be a constant protectress of my whole life, and my faithful guide. Turn thy eyes, thy mild eyes, at all times, with compassion on me. Watch over me like a mother in every temptation. Protect me faithfully against my enemies, protect me beneath thy tender arms. Let thy faithful kissing of His wounds be to me as a tender reconciliation with Him; Let the wounds of thy heart obtain for me a cordial repentance of my sins; Thy fervent sighing procure for me a constant yearning; And let thy bitter tears soften my hard heart; Be thy lamentable words even as a renunciation to me of all voluptuous speeches; Thy weeping form as a casting away of all dissolute conduct; Thy disconsolate heart as a despising of all perishable affections.

# ON SATURDAY, OR AT COMPLINE

O, Thou ravishing brightness of eternal light, how art Thou at this moment, when my soul embraces Thee under the cross as dead in Thy sorrowful mother's lap, with lamentations and thanksgiving, how art Thou utterly extinguished! Extinguish in me the burning desire of all vice. 2. O, Thou pure clear mirror of the Divine Majesty, how art Thou defiled for very love of me! Wash out the great stains of my evil deeds. 3. O, fair and shining Image of the Fatherly goodness, how grievously disfigured Thou art! Restore the disfigured image of my soul. 4. O, innocent Lamb, how piteously art Thou abased! Atone and reform for me my guilty sinful life. 5. O, King of all kings, O, Lord of all lords, vouchsafe me, since my soul embraces Thee with sorrow and lamentation in Thy abasement, that it may be embraced by Thee with joy in Thy eternal glory. O, pure Mother, worthy of all love, remember to-day, 1. The forlorn condition in which thou foundest thyself when they tore thy murdered Son from thy breast; 2. Remember thy separation from Him; 3. Thy faltering steps; 4. Thy heart sighing again for His body; 5. The constant fidelity which thou alone didst evince for Him in all His woe till He was laid in the grave. Obtain for me, from thy tender Son, that in thy sorrow and His sufferings I may subdue my own. Moreover, that I may shut myself up with Him in His sepulchre from all temporal anxieties; That I may be inspired with disgust for all this world; That I may only cherish a perpetual desire of Him, and may persevere in His praise and service to the grave. Amen.

*When all this was ready and written out, there still remained a little to make up at the end of a chapter, appertaining to our Blessed Lady, and in that very part he had left a blank space until he should be inspired with it by God, for he had been many months in a state of spiritual dereliction, so that he could not finish the chapter. Then he besought our Blessed Lady, the Mother of God, that she would do it. And, on the eve of St. Dominic, at night, after he had sung matins, it seemed to him in his sleep, as if he were in a chamber; and as if, while he was sitting there, a very fair youth entered with a ravishing harp, and with him* four other youths with flutes. Then the youth with the harp sat down by the brother, and began to touch his harp, and play upon it very sweetly. This was pleasant for the brother to hear, and he said to him, O, when wilt thou come to the place where I dwell, and lift up my heart a little with thy music? Then the youth asked the brother if he was still busy with what he had for a long time been occupied with? To which he said, Yes. Then the youth answered and said: It is hard to play. So he turned to the four with flutes, and bid them blow. Then one of them answered and said that if two of them blew it would be enough. But the other said, that two would not be enough, and that they must all blow their flutes together, and he gave them a certain tune, which was well known to him, but of which the brother knew nothing, and it was done accordingly.

Meanwhile he presently neither saw nor heard any harp or flute, but saw that the youths had in their hands a picture, above all measure lovely, of our Blessed Lady, and that it was worked in cloth, and the mantle of the picture was red and purple, with damask embroidery, which it was delightful to behold, and the ground was as white as snow. Then the brother marvelled greatly, and took pleasure in the sight; and he perceived that they would needs complete it, and, first of all, fill up the empty space. Then they said, See how it grows! Presently he saw it completed. And then one of them took a needle and thread, and made on the fore part of the mantle very skillful cross stitches, and *they were very finely done, and wonderfully adorned our Blessed Lady. And now his eyes were opened, and he understood that he should no longer doubt that it was given him to complete the ground, the blank space, and the spiritual picture, which had so long been denied to him; for he was accustomed to have all that he had hitherto performed clearly manifested to him by God in the way of some similitude like the above, and so, on the morrow, he finished his work to the end.*

Copyright © 2024 by SSEL
*Scribere Semper Et Legere*
Cover design : Canva.com
Painting : *Heinrich Seuse*, Francisco de Zurbaran, 1638, Museo de Bellas Artes de Sevilla.
Ebook ISBN 979-10-299-1722-6
Paperback ISBN 979-10-299-1723-3
Hardcover ISBN 979-10-299-1724-0
All rights reserved.

www.ingramcontent.com/pod-product-compliance
Lightning Source LLC
LaVergne TN
LVHW030311070526
838199LV00007B/372